About the TLS

The *Times Literary Supplement* was born in January 1902. Its first ever front page bashfully stated that 'during the Parliamentary session Literary Supplements to "The Times" will appear as often as may be necessary in order to keep abreast with the more important publications of the day'. Fortunately, the question of necessity was not left in the hands of literary journalists (who, we can imagine, might occasionally push for a holiday or two), and the title became a weekly one. A few years later, the *TLS* split entirely from *The Times*.

Since then, we have prided ourselves on being the world's leading magazine for culture and ideas. Our guiding principle for the selection of pieces remains the same as it ever has been: is it interesting; and is it beautifully written? Over the years, our contributors have included the very best writers and thinkers in the world: from

Virginia Woolf to Seamus Heaney, Sylvia Plath to Susan Sontag, Milan Kundera to Christopher Hitchens, Patricia Highsmith to Martin Scorsese.

The book you are holding is part of a brand-new imprint, *TLS Books*, by which we are striving to bring more beautiful writing to a wider public. We hope you enjoy it. If you want to read more from us, you'll find a special trial subscription offer to the *TLS* at the back of this book.

In an ever-quickening culture of flipness and facility, fake news and Facebook, the *TLS* is determined to be part of the counter-culture of quality. We believe in expertise, breadth and depth. We believe in the importance of ideas, and the transformative power of art. And we believe that, in reading the *TLS* – in whatever form, be it in a magazine, online or in a book – you are supporting a set of values that we have been proud to uphold for more than a hundred years. So thank you for that.

Stig Abell, 11th Editor of the *TLS*
London, 2019

The Imaginary Museum

The Imaginary Museum

A personal tour of contemporary art featuring ghosts, nudity and disagreements

Ben Eastham

TLS

TLS Books
An imprint of HarperCollins*Publishers*
1 London Bridge Street
London SE1 9GF

The-TLS.co.uk

First published in Great Britain in 2020 by TLS Books

1

A catalogue record for this book is
available from the British Library

ISBN 978-0-00-837542-3

Typeset in Publico Text
Printed and bound in Great Britain by
CPI Group (UK) Ltd, Croydon

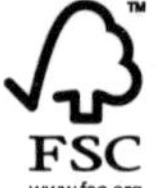

Just as we should view art not as an
accumulation of so-called art objects,
but as a way of approaching knowledge,
we should also view knowledge not as an
accumulation of data, but as a flexible
mechanism for reorganizing reality
– *Luis Camnitzer*

Museums are just a lot of lies
– *Pablo Picasso*

Introduction

'Great nations write their autobiographies in three manuscripts', wrote John Ruskin, 'the book of their deeds, the book of their words and the book of their art.' Which begs the question: what does the book of contemporary art tell us about the society in which we live today? How should you read it and who gets to write it?

These questions came to mind when, on my first assignment as an art critic, I watched a naked man climb slowly onto a jet engine. Once he had reached his perch and assumed the pose of Rodin's *The Thinker*, a curator explained to the press gathered around the jet that this performance signified England's retreat into post-industrial nostalgia. The nude redoubled his attempts to look nostalgic while, beneath him, several critics nodded to signal that this only confirmed what they had already intuited. I raised my pen to announce to my competitors the imminent arrival of a brilliant critical insight and, when it failed to appear, was reduced to sketching a cartoon penis into my notebook.

There was more of this in the exhibition: a stack of tightly rolled hotel towels alluding, we were told, to the international art world's fantastically high carbon footprint; battered computer hard drives highlighting China's exploitation of Africa's natural resources. I had no idea what to make of all this and so, when the press preview came to an end, was eager to dodge the mingling over coffee and pastries for fear of being caught out in conversation by someone who did. Having pocketed a miniature croissant, my escape was thwarted when I bumped into the arts correspondent of a national newspaper rolling a cigarette at the door.

I said sorry and then, in the hope of gleaning some idea I could plagiarize for my own review, asked him what he made of the show.

'No fucking idea', he replied. 'Who are you?'

I told him my name.

He patted his pockets for a lighter, found it, cupped the flame to his lips. 'I liked it, though', he said. Then, after a pause, 'You?'

Ruskin's quote continues: 'Not one of these books [of a nation's deeds, words, art] can be understood unless we read the two others, but of the three the only trustworthy one is the last.' You don't have to like what it says, the Victorian art critic tells us, but the book of art does not lie. If it seems that art strayed a few decades ago into illegibility, then it might be that the book doesn't only document the state of nations but predicts them.

Because the stories that have shaped western societies since the fall of the Berlin Wall seem recently to have broken down: it is no longer possible to assume the 'end of history' through the inevitable triumph of liberal democracy, free-market capitalism and human rights-based law. Financial crises, mass migrations, global pandemics and environmental catastrophes have, what's more, revealed the systems governing our lives to be complicated beyond the comprehension of even those tasked with managing them. From the ex-chairman of the US Federal Reserve conceding that the subprime mortgage crisis had undermined his basic faith in 'the way the world works', to scientists reiterating that the global ecosystem is so entangled that the local effects of climate change cannot accurately be foreseen, or world leaders being forced by an unruly strand of ribonucleic acid to incarcerate whole populations, the old authorities appear to have lost control of the narrative.

The effects are exacerbated by our access to unprecedented amounts of data while remaining unschooled in how to filter it. We are drowning in information that we are no longer able to organize into easily comprehensible stories. Disbarred from conversations we are told are beyond us, it's not surprising that so many succumb to scapegoating and the seductions of populists who abuse 'plain' speech and appeal to 'simpler' pasts. There is a prevailing sense, in the west, of the thread that binds communities together having unravelled.

It is a staple criticism of contemporary art that it, too, has lost the plot. In the past couple of years I have attended a seven-hour-recital of a looping two-and-half-minute passage from Franz Schubert's 'An die Musik'; travelled via virtual reality simulation to the surface of the moon not once but twice; watched an opera about climate change set on an artificial beach in an Italian military complex; taken a lesson in Sinhalese at a Manchester museum; and chaired a discussion about a video set in a Silicon Valley dystopia featuring a transgender dancer who brings Ayn Rand to climax. That all of these events have been framed as art could be taken as evidence that the term has lost all meaning, or that it has become so highly coded as to be indecipherable to anyone without a specialist education. It's easy to imagine eyes rolling, but I found all of the above experiences in some way moving, memorable or enlightening. New forms of art – going back to Impressionism and beyond – have routinely been dismissed as absurd, the speculation of chancers or the ravings of the deranged. So it is worth asking: what binds together these and other works of contemporary art? And how do they reflect on a complex and chaotic world?

What we call contemporary art is conventionally dated from the late 1960s, when it succeeded modern art, but is better understood as a style than an era. Where movements have historically been defined by shared forms and subjects linked to their sponsors (church, state, merchants), the art of today can only loosely be identified by some common characteristics: it foregrounds ideas over forms and materials; borrows liberally and not always responsibly from disciplines as varied as philosophy, ecology and sociology; is preoccupied by forming connections between disparate ideas and cultures; is sceptical of received wisdoms; takes place in a globalized world; is, to quote Marshall McLuhan, 'whatever you can get away with' or, to paraphrase Robert Rauschenberg, 'whatever I say it is'.

Indeed, it's easier to conclude that 'the only definition of art', as the American conceptual artist Joseph Kosuth put it, 'is art'. Which is another way of saying that art is not a theory, it's an activity. And, by extension, that art today is less about the formal or aesthetic properties of an object than a way of talking about the intricately entangled, increasingly unstable world in which we live.

All this talk about art being 'whatever you make of it' may sound flippant, but was intended to make art more accessible. If art is a conversation about the societies in which we live, then everyone in a democracy is entitled to an opinion and should be free to express it. However, instead of clearing the air, the claim has been harnessed by those with a vested interest in maintaining a mystique around art. This atmosphere has suffocated many early engagements with art, including my own.

As a more or less pretentious teenager in a small town at the turn of the twenty-first century, I thought of modern and contemporary art as of an exotic animal: I was eager to see it, confident I could recognize it, certain it couldn't be found in market towns on the Welsh borders. Yet the excitement of visiting museums in Liverpool or London was always tempered by the suspicion that I was getting it wrong. Why did I find Rachel Whiteread's minimalist sculptures so compelling and Mark Rothko's paintings so unrewarding? I was bored by paintings that I had expected to prompt some kind of divine revelation and this felt like an indictment of my own irredeemably provincial taste. It was easy to allow that failure to settle into cynicism. Could all these people *really* be seeing God in blurred fields of black and red? Instead of attending to the work, I drifted into speculations on art and suggestibility.

Two decades on, I can better appreciate the technical accomplishment of Rothko's paintings and their significance within a history of western art, but they still don't really do it for me. No doubt in a decade I will break down in tears in front of some Rothko, realize that my previous indifference was a symptom of my own emotional immaturity and regret committing the above sentences to print. But you shouldn't force it, and you can't pretend. That these paintings don't move me now isn't to deny that they move others and may move a future version of myself. What interests me is the combination of individual personality, wider circumstances and work of art that generates those effects.

I started this essay with the brief conversation with a critic because it offers a way of looking at art. Put bluntly, you sometimes need to acknowledge that you have no fucking idea what you're looking at. Instead of worrying about not getting it, attend to your feelings and then afterwards try and figure out what catalysed that reaction. The critic's admission that he was bewildered was intended, I think, to make me feel comfortable about articulating my own opinion without fearing that this would be held against me. Not understanding is, after all, a precondition of learning something new.

Indeed, bewilderment has a proud intellectual history. Let's start, for the sake of variety, with the second-century theologian St Gregory the Illuminator. Credited with curing King Tiridates of the unkingly delusion that he was a boar, Gregory warned that 'we make idols of our concepts, but wisdom is born of wonder'. In *Against Interpretation* (1966), a more familiar source for contemporary art criticism, Susan Sontag argued that we must allow works of art to act on our senses before imposing theoretical constructs upon them (calling, memorably, for 'an erotics of art'). Iris Murdoch agreed that not all experience should be reduced to an analytic exercise, arguing that philosophy must accommodate 'the smell of the Paris metro or what it is like to hold a mouse in one's hand'. The great American painter Ed Ruscha summarized this very Proustian idea in a more Californian idiom: a good work of art, he said, provokes the reaction 'Huh? Wow!' and a bad one the anticlimactic 'Wow! Huh?' In other words, if you can't make head or tail of a work of art but nonetheless feel something towards it – attraction or repulsion, delight or rage, wonder or confusion – you're halfway to having a meaningful experience of it. (And a lot closer than anyone who claims to have it all worked out beforehand.)

We should not be intimidated by uncertainty, but embrace it. For while it can be useful to know the names of paintings, their dates and schools, and the biographies of the artists, it is never sufficient. I can identify Beatriz González's *Interior Decoration* (1981) at a glance; I can tell you that it is a twenty-metre-long section of screen-printed fabric that hangs from a curtain rail; that it depicts and condemns a corrupt Colombian president and his coterie; can describe the influence of American Pop on its stylized figures even as it critiques the cultural imperialism that Pop seems to cele-brate; can speculate on the influence on the artist of radical German and Italian art of the 1970s; can relate the work to art's political purpose in Latin America. And yet none of this means in any significant sense that I know the painting. If I did, I wouldn't have had to traipse across the Thames to the Tate Modern to look at it.

This is what we mean, I think, when we say carelessly that a work of art is 'timeless'. Not that an artwork encodes some single abiding truth that only a priestly class can discern, but rather that it rewards different interpretations as the world changes around it. I keep returning to González's work not to experience the same reaction to its patterns and colours, but because I anticipate a different one. As such, it offers a yardstick against which to gauge how I, and the world of which I am a part, have shifted. The 'meaning' of a painting, like the 'meaning' of the world, emerges through your encounter with it.

A prosaic example: as a moody adolescent I loved the early sculptures of Damien Hirst. I was exhilarated by *Mother and Child (Divided)* (1993), which preserves the bisected bodies of a cow and her calf in four glass vitrines filled with clear formaldehyde, and *A Thousand Years* (1990), two glass cages containing a severed cow's head fed on by maggots which metamorphose into flies before their electrocution by a dangling bug zapper. That I now find Hirst's works tiresome isn't because they have changed; it's because I and the times have. An energetic disregard for taste and tradition that when I was younger and caught up in the sanctioned rebellions of Cool Britannia seemed puckish now feels derivative and, in the context of species extinction and deadly pandemics, ostentatiously cruel. I'd like to talk the works over with my younger self, although I suspect his spiky enthusiasm might win out over my dim disillusion.

I could tell him why Hirst's work is less politically engaged than his Italian predecessors in Arte Povera, but I doubt such an argument (which he would dismiss as snobbish) would

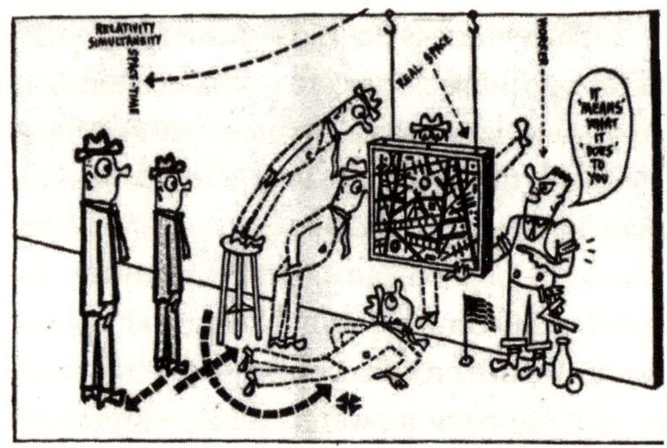

change his mind and I'm not sure it should. I value the potential of a work to prompt new and constructive ways of thinking, he values its challenge to conventions of good taste. I like jazz; he *hates* jazz. Talking about art, as about any subject that isn't governed by a written constitution, requires that both parties acknowledge that they might be judging the same thing by different metrics, in the light of personal experiences foreign to the other, and that neither has access to the absolute truth of an artwork: it doesn't exist.

Because there is no 'right' place from which to look at things. The cartoon opposite by the great American abstract painter Ad Reinhardt literalizes this principle: in it, a neatly dressed man is trying to find the correct spot from which to observe an abstract painting. He shuffles in front of, around and behind the canvas, stands on a chair and crawls underneath it, as if the painting were a magic-eye illusion from which a vase and flowers emerges if you squint the right way. A technician holding the painting, irritated by his nervous shuffling about, shouts out some good advice: 'It "means" what it "does" to you!'

It's worth making clear – before I'm accused of reducing the appreciation of art to knee-jerk emotional reaction or radical relativism – that this does not relieve viewers of the responsibility to reflect on *why* the work does what it does to them. Quite the opposite: self-interrogation, which is a step in the direction of self-knowledge, seems to me pretty much the whole point of looking at art. Why does this jumble of shapes and colours make me feel happy or alienated or seen? What does the response reveal of my own (unexamined) prejudices, my own state of mind? If you are charmed by a video work which collages together clips of cats playing on the piano, or irritated by a stack of broken televisions, or thrilled by a nineteenth-century painting of an idyllic landscape, what does that tell you about yourself in relation to the society that sees fit to put those works in museums?

Returning to that chance encounter with the art critic, I wish I could say that I admitted to having no idea what was going on either, and that we decamped to a pub to discuss what jet engines mean to us (symbols of industrial might or catalysts of environmental catastrophe?) and why. But, in truth, I said something closer to, 'Yeah, it seemed to me that the underlying conceptual frameworks were interesting, but that the choreography of the space was mishandled', which is just the kind of nonsense that bad critics deliver when attempting to scaffold pure wind. Recognizing that I wanted to cut the conversation short, the critic shrugged and trained his attention on the floor while I scurried off shamefacedly in the hope that he wouldn't remember my name (he didn't).

The people who are really good at making, curating and writing about art are those who are willing to acknowledge their own ignorance. I don't mean that all critics, art historians and curators are bluffers, nor that artists are setting out deliberately to make impenetrable work (some of them do it by accident). Nor do I mean that there is no 'good' or 'bad' art: an afternoon at a contemporary art fair would disabuse anyone of that idea. I mean only that every discipline based on enquiry depends on the study of things that its specialists can't explain away. Good art has always raised difficult questions, offended taste and challenged established categories.

So we should resist the urge to box a work of art into a school, movement or style and in doing so to identify it by its category rather than on its own terms. This seems to me an ethical principle, because works of art are not fully knowable any more than people are fully knowable. I often think of a scene in Federico Fellini's *8½* (1963). A film theorist brought in to advise the director on his script laments 'the ambiguity, the confusion' of a story which, because it is based on the director's own life, lacks 'a clear philosophy'. But the joke is on the theorist: neither art nor people are reducible to 'a clear philosophy'.

If the meaning of a work of art is shaped by the circumstances in which it is received as well as those in which it was made – look at a painting like Diego Velázquez's *Las Meninas* (1656), for instance, and see how what it means is renegotiated by each new generation of viewers – then reading the book of art, following Ruskin, also helps us to understand ourselves and others. In contemporary Britain, looking at art offers an opportunity to talk (at the safety of one remove) about who we are individually and collectively, how those identities are shaped and on what stories they are founded.

Those conversations take place in galleries and museums, between works of art from different eras and places, and people with diverse opinions. And so, thinking about how to introduce the idea of art as an open and ongoing conversation, I imagined the rest of this essay as an art museum through which I would walk the reader. This project was made unexpectedly timely by a global health emergency that suddenly made it impossible to trip to the Tate or to any other museum, forcing us all to retreat into the stacks and storerooms of our memories.

It transpired that my mind is a shambles, and so my imaginary museum is not structured as its bricks-and-mortar equivalents must be. Instead of such practicalities as load-bearing walls and Euclidean dimensions, this institution is riddled with secret passageways and trapdoors. There are moving walls and hidden floors, and the interior observes a flexible relationship to time and space. Like my mind, the museum is full of people, some of whom are welcome and some of whom are not.

This short essay is not, I should make clear, an attempt to construct an authoritative or remotely coherent overview of contemporary art. Instead it is an exercise in trying to construct a story from the materials available to me, which is to say the works of art at the top of my head. It hopes to demonstrate that the history of art is not a long line of masterpieces stretching back hundreds of years but an evolving dialogue – with other works of art, with society, with the history of ideas, with other people – in which everyone should feel able to participate. So let me take you on a tour of the art collection that I keep in my mind and tell you a story that I hope you'll contest.

Ground Floor

Before we enter the museum, let's pause briefly on the street – imagine a once-grand neighbour-hood, now fallen into disrepair, in a minor European city – and observe three black bin bags slouched against the building's wall. I first saw these rumpled sacks outside an exhibition at the Venice Biennale, and took pleasure in watching two hipsters excitedly taking pictures of them in the mistaken assumption that they were art. It was only when I noticed a sign on the wall, having already worked this scene into a satirical column on art in the age of Instagram, that I learned that the bags were, in fact, carved with extraordinary skill from blocks of black marble. Which is to say, the joke was on me. I keep these *trompe l'œil* sculptures by the Greek artist Andreas Lolis at the entrance to my imaginary museum as a warning against making snap judgements, and as a pre-emptive strike against the accusation that contemporary art is rubbish.

Let's walk up the short flight of steps leading to the museum entrance (it is open twenty-four hours a day, and if you've bought this book you've paid the entrance fee). Beyond the threshold we move into a high-ceilinged marble atrium that buzzes with the chatter of the people inside. Running along the floor are three painted lines – red, yellow and green – which branch in different directions as they travel into the space ahead. We'll follow the red one, taking us under a series of square metal chandeliers festooned with neon bulbs that light up as we pass beneath, while around us visitors sit on long benches upholstered in harlequin fabrics. The red line ends in front of a set of double doors – I wave away the inspector who asks to see our tickets – through which we enter a bright and quiet gallery. On the concrete floor is a pair of spectacles. A knot of people has formed around it.

As you might have guessed, this isn't really a work of art. In homage to a practical joke played by students at the San Francisco

Museum of Modern Art in 2016, I've placed this ordinary pair of glasses onto the floor in order to test a basic theory, namely that people expect to see art when they enter a museum and treat everything they encounter as such. It's a reasonable assumption, and I'm not exempt from the misapprehension it causes: I took the sculptures by Andreas Lolis for refuse because they *weren't* in a museum. Here's the first lesson of contemporary art: we attend to

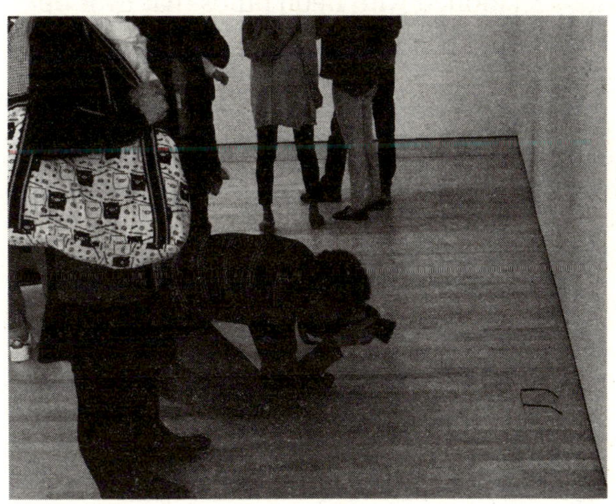

objects and images differently depending on where and in what state of mind we meet them.

The special way of seeing that we reserve for museums is, unless you are the kind of person who goes to a museum to complain about it, an open and rewarding one. If, to take the example at hand, you really *look* at spectacles it's difficult not to be struck by how marvellous they are. The aesthetically pleasing ellipses into which the lenses have been cut are a triumph of human craft; that spectacles are the first wearable technology is interesting in the context of a discussion about how we see things. This relationship between art and the everyday world works both ways: after seeing Lolis's imitation bin bags I started noticing real ones on the streets of Venice, meaning that I spent much of the day on which I was supposed to be writing a review contemplating the vast amount of waste produced in making a major exhibition. These are examples of how art takes us outside the frame of its own reference, and how contemporary art depends in large part for its meaning on its contexts.

This reliance on context is apt to irritate those who think that art should be identifiable as such by how it looks and of what it is made. The art critic Robert Hughes pointed out that if you were to take the pile of bricks that comprises Carl Andre's minimalist sculpture *Equivalent VIII* (1966) out of the museum and place it in a parking lot, it would no longer be a work of art but a neat stack of building materials. If you were to put a sculpture by Rodin in a parking lot, by contrast, it would be a 'misplaced' work of art. Hughes was emphasizing that the Rodin is identified as art by its form, while the Andre (which Hughes also admired) is identified as art by the idea behind it. For all that I have issues with this tendency to draw battle lines between form and content, to trust in the aura of an artwork and to assume that art should be found in museums and never parking lots, it does identify a useful distinction: a large part of the contemporary art I like does not aspire to independence from the everyday world but to alert us to it.

Because we don't pay attention to things. This is more rather than less true of those who pride themselves on their credentials as art lovers. In *The Painter of Modern Life*, Charles Baudelaire rails against the nineteenth-century culture vultures who 'go to the Louvre, walk rapidly, without so much as a glance' past dozens of less celebrated but potentially rewarding paintings to stand in front of their favourite 'masterpiece' (Baudelaire cites Titian,

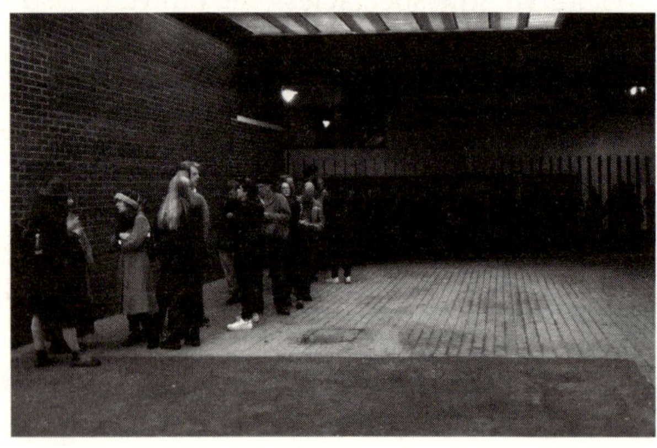

but you might swap in Frida Kahlo or Gerhard Richter) then 'go home happy, not a few saying to themselves, "I know my museum"'. Baudelaire, who sought out beauty on the street and in unexpected places, disdains those who recognize art only where they have been reliably informed it exists in its highest concentration. Anyone who has been recently to the Louvre and stood at the back of the crowd of people holding phones over their heads to take pictures of the distant 'Mona Lisa' will sympathize with the poet's irritation.

But we've already spent too much time in the vicinity of the spectacles. The crowd of people is growing, and I don't want them to waste their time on a silly prank when they could be spending it with the really important works of art in the next room. I'll go over and pick up the errant specs.

As I'm leaning down, a security guard taps me on the shoulder.

'Excuse me, sir. Please do not touch the work.'

Oh, how funny.

I am pleased to see that this security guard is, judging from the profound humourlessness etched into his face, from the old school of uniformed pedants who carry a whistle and search out reasons to use it. Just the kind of person, in short, I want looking after my collection.

'Hello there!' I say, in the bright tone of a director who would make it clear that he is as comfortable chatting with the staff as, say, the head of charitable giving at British Petroleum.

Neither recognition nor awe brightens his face.

'I'm the director', I clarify.

'Very good to meet you, sir.'

'Likewise. Look, funny thing, I put these spectacles down to illustrate a point to my reader here. Just a joke, really. But it's got a bit out of hand and now these people are getting in everyone's way.'

'You cannot touch the work of art, sir.'

'Sorry, what?'

'Sir, the work of art cannot be touched.'

'Yes, that's just the same sentence backwards. I understand the principle. But the specs are not a work of art.'

'Yes, they are.'

'No, they're not.'

He lets the air slowly out of his chest and informs me sadly, as if he would love to have this conversation if he were less busy, that we are not going to have this conversation.

I say that we are going to have this conversation, at which he waves stiffly across the gallery to a man in round glasses. Not young, and yet not sufficiently old to accept with dignity that he is bald, this is a curator. He walks over and looks me up and down.

'Is there a problem?'

'Good, you can sort this out. I've asked this guard to remove this obstacle and he's refusing.'

The curator ducks his head, quizzically.

'I'm the director?' I clarify.

He touches his fingers to his lips, smiles and says, 'Well, you see, that's a work of art.'

'No it's not.'

He looks over the top of his glasses.

'I think you'll find that this work is part of a theoretical tradition stretching back to Marcel Duchamp's urinal, the *seminal*', curators often speak in italics and use the wrong word, 'example of found art ...'.

The guard interrupts.

'I used to guard that urinal at the Tate. And – you know – people once said that it wasn't a work of art. But now everyone knows that it is.'

'In fact', says the curator, 'even the committee organizing the exhibition where it first appeared thought that the urinal wasn't a work of art. But they were *wrong*. Indeed, the funny thing is that even if you *were* the director', he raises his eyebrows, 'it wouldn't mean you're *right* about the spectacles. Quite amusing really.'

'But Duchamp was exploiting', and here my voice breaks, embarrassingly, 'a loophole in the definition of art. The committee was contractually obliged to accept as art whatever he put into the exhibition. That's what makes it such a good joke. That and the fact that it went on to be the most influential work of art in the twentieth century. Anyway, his friend Alfred Stieglitz threw away the urinal afterwards. The artwork is the idea, which is to say the joke. The urinal doesn't matter.'

'Well that's what you say', retorts the guard, 'but the tour guides in the Tate were always complaining that they only had a copy of the urinal because that idiot threw the original away. If you had it now it would be worth millions! What if these spectacles end up being worth millions, eh? And you've gone and thrown them away? Not on my watch!'

The curator rolls his eyes and starts talking about phenomenological presence and Maurice Merleau-Ponty, which is what curators do when they get flustered. I've had enough of this.

'You know, this whole museum is my own invention. We're actually *in my mind*. Which means', I look meaningfully at the pair of them, at the crowd around us, 'that you only exist in my imagination. I could just ...'.

I click my fingers.

'... poof'.

The security guard reaches for his walkie-talkie.

I click my fingers. I click my fingers again.

The guard reaches for his holster.

Fuck.

I run over to the spectacles, jump up and down on them and grind them under my heel.

While they're freaking out about the spectacles, we can hotfoot it down this corridor. See that big stone fireplace? Just stand by the coal scuttle while I pull at this poker, the gears are crunching, hold on ...

First Floor

I knew that revolving door would come in handy. From here we can take the service passageways to the backstairs that lead up to the next floor. But now that we're moving through those parts of the building not open to the public, some house rules. Open doors through which a curiously seductive void can be glimpsed should not be entered. The same applies to any cupboards from which you hear any banging, shaking, banshee-wailing. If you encounter a gathering black cloud, run away. I don't know for sure what's buried in some of the more remote corners of the museum, and I don't want to find out.

That drama with the security guard means, I'm sorry to say, that we missed a number of masterpieces on the museum's ground floor. There are paintings by Sindoedarsono Sudjojono that illustrate a clever point I was planning to make about how ideas travel between cultures and adapt to local contexts, a set of mannequins wearing the costumes that Oskar Schlemmer designed for the Bauhaus ballet. There is a room filled with poetry and another filled with pots from a museum in Athens alongside vases by Michael Frimkess and Magdalena Suarez Frimkess. You'll just have to look out for them in the real world.

Coming up through the innards of the museum will take us straight into the gallery dedicated to Tino Sehgal's *This Variation* (2012). I first came across this difficult-to-classify work of art at Documenta, a vast exhibition of contemporary art which takes place every five years in the German city of Kassel. The city has been shaped by the legacy of these festivals: the oak trees that line its streets, to take one example, were planted as part of the conceptual artist, Olympian bullshitter and cofounder of Germany's Green Party Joseph Beuys's contribution to the 1982 edition (the work is titled, sensibly enough, *7,000 oak trees*). The consequence of all these interventions is that it is sometimes hard to be sure, as you walk through the city, whether you're passing a bus stop or a work of art.

There is no reason, of course, that a plastic shelter can't be both. But I didn't think like that at the time, and so instead spent much of my visit worrying that I might make a fool of myself in front of my more sophisticated friend by mistaking a set of kitschy garden gnomes for the work of a Japanese Pop artist. To avoid doing so, I started a running gag in which I would point things out that might, by virtue of looking a bit weird, be 'art' (or in German, *kunst*). Thus, an abandoned sex shop became 'installation *kunst*'; a woman gesticulating with a rubber chicken towards a man in a bar was 'feminist performance *kunst*'; a car alarm

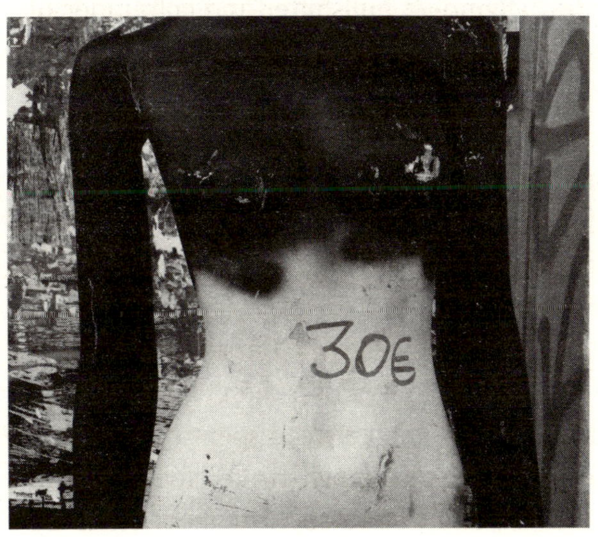

outside an exhibition venue must be 'protest *kunst*'. And it was while playing this game, walking down a narrow alleyway and into a sunlit courtyard, that we chanced on a curtained doorway like the one that – having reached the top of the museum's backstairs – we find before us now.

Through the curtains is a darkness so complete as to have its own weight and texture. Resist the temptation to retreat back through the blackout drapes and into the light, and after a few seconds you feel a pressure on your elbow that runs down your forearm and resolves into a hand which pulls you a few steps further into the black. A woman's voice strikes up, and the shape of the sound suggests that we're in a space of roughly the same dimensions as a school classroom. She tells a story about the end of a relationship – about falling out of love – and, when she finishes, someone starts to sing. Your eyes are adjusting, and so the undifferentiated blackness complicates into grey patterns. Now that you can make out the silhouettes of other people in the room, we make our way to its edge and sit down on the floor with our backs against the wall. More people tell stories, some sing and are joined by the voices of others. If you look to the door you can watch the new arrivals stand blindly on the threshold, while other audience members whose eyes have adapted take their hands and lead them through the room. If you choose, you too can tell a story to the audience or take up the role of a guide.

One of the issues with museums of the mind is that they are soon invaded by people you know and were trying to forget. I can see a woman I've barred from my private institution. She's over there, with the long features, quizzical expression and musical gait. She's a menace. She's always poking around in store rooms; talking through film screenings; moving works of art around or hiding them from me. Now she lifts her head and starts softly to sing in a language I don't understand. I'm going to have to leave. You stay here for as long as you want, I'll meet you on the other side of the curtain.

Ah, there you are, sorry about that. Anyway, what did you think of Sehgal's work? When I first entered that darkness years ago, I remember my anxiety about what qualified as art melting away. I was grateful at first simply to be guided through this unlit space and then to listen to the stories, some of which were delivered by performers working with the artist, others offered spontaneously by members of the audience. By making me feel vulnerable – by forcing me, in effect, to suspend my cynicism and to accept the assistance of volunteers – that dark room made me unusually receptive to what happened inside it. When I came out of it into the light of the world, I felt that the dust had been washed from my eyes.

Second Floor

Sehgal describes his works of participatory theatre, music, or dance, as 'constructed situations', which is one way of thinking about how we experience art. Less like a lecture – in which you listen dutifully to what the artist has to tell you – than a conversation to which you are invited to contribute. That dialogue extends to include other people, whether the friends you saw it with or in the books you read about it. To explore the idea of art as a space in which to listen and also to speak, let's take the elevator to the museum's second floor. Here I've built an amphitheatre for symposia, film screenings, theatrical performances, poetry readings, dance and all the other cultural activities that have in recent decades been folded into the remit of a contemporary art museum.

From the elevator we move through a busy concourse into an L-shaped gallery that doubles as an anteroom for the concert hall. On a long wall hangs a three-metre-wide painting by Lubaina Himid, titled *Six Tailors* (2019). It shows five black men gathered around a table laid with the tools of their trade: strips of gingham check fabric, spools of cotton thread and curved pattern cutters. Another man walks behind the tailors, all of whom wear brightly coloured clothes with the conspicuous exception of one ghostly grey figure. The composition of the picture is strictly geometrical: halfway up the canvas, a saffron floor meets a straw-yellow back wall intersected by a narrow rectangular window through which can be seen a grey and restless sea; the table is distorted by perspective into a turquoise trapezoid that extends out to the bottom of the frame. These planes of solid colour contrast with the highly individualized rendering of the characters' black faces. Himid, who often paints seascapes glimpsed through the windows of interior scenes, has spoken of these bodies of water as alluding specifically to the history of slavery. Which is to say, more broadly, that the fictional spaces in which paintings happen aren't perfectly sealed off from the world.

The same is true of the scene depicted in this painting. Pictured in steep perspective, the tailors' working table threatens to jut out into the real (well, kind of) space of the room in which we're standing. One of the tailors looks out expectantly at the viewer. Which prompts the question, depending on how you interpret the figures in the painting (and there's a lot going on here), of whether you might be the titular sixth tailor. And, if so, what are you bringing to the table? Himid, whose mother was a textile designer and whose own background is in set design, has pointed out that the battery of instruments on the table is not complete. It's an open invitation to lend your skills and your tools to the production of something new.

The labour of completing an artwork is shared between artist and audience, and so the painting cannot be understood independently from its observer. This isn't, I should make clear, a new idea: artists have been jumping out of the picture plane for centuries, whether by painting the hands of their subjects creeping out over the frame or by playing with the scenery to suggest a drape pulled back for the benefit of the viewer. But I've included this work to make clear that paintings as much as performances can enlist the viewer in the construction of an artwork's meaning. It's a mistake to assume that because a painting might look more like a work of art from the past that it must share its principles, a little like the 'false friends' that one encounters in translating one language into another. Himid's work, it seems to me, has more in common with *This Variation* than with any number of paintings that it might more superficially resemble. But enough of that, because the bell is ringing to signal the start of the performance, so let's follow these people into the auditorium.

Behind a stage occupied by a single grand piano is a screen onto which a beam of white

light is projected, its bottom edge crenellated by the shadows of people's heads as they take their seats. When quiet has descended, a musician in a black dress enters from stage right. She sits at the piano, composes herself, opens the lid and lowers her arms to her sides. Nothing happens. The quiet rumble of traffic from the street outside becomes audible, and soon what seemed like perfect silence is revealed to be a medley of shuffles, coughs and suppressed sneezes. John Cage has said that any sound occurring within the four minutes and thirty-three seconds of his notorious 'silent' composition should be understood as part of the work. The members of the audience are transformed into artists, no matter that their contributions are here limited to a hurriedly extinguished ringtone. If you pay close attention to the white screen you might make out the flickering silhouettes of insects caught in the projector's beam, or an arm raised up to the ceiling in a stretch.

People gathering in an auditorium to listen to the sound of their own discomfort is, let's be honest, pretty funny. That I am stifling a giggle would not, I think, have irritated Cage. If you doubt me, go to YouTube and watch him perform his composition 'Water Walk' on the televised variety show *I've Got a Secret* in 1960: in front of a hysterical studio audience, the great vanguard artist runs around banging pots, boiling kettles, dropping radios and, all in all, having a lot of fun. In fact, humour is the most undervalued element in art, which I've always understood as being fundamentally about play.

Friedrich Schiller had this mapped out two hundred years ago ... but, hang on, there's a commotion at the side of the stage. It's the security guard again, his chest all puffed out like he's on the trail of the Maltese Falcon. He's clambering up onto the stage, carrying a megaphone. Oh, he is going to make an announcement ...

'Ladies and Gentlemen', his amplified voice crackles. 'There is among us an intruder, bent on destruction. He is suffering from delusions and should only be approached by those with an intimate understanding of the criminal mind, like me. The suspect has a hostage. The suspect is taller than people seem to think. If you see a man matching this description – please – alert me immediately. Do not be alarmed, you are in good hands. Enjoy the rest of the performance.'

And with that, our aspiring Dick Tracy clambers offstage.

The pianist, who has paid no attention to the interruption, sits without moving for another minute or so before delicately closing the lid on her instrument, accepting the applause and exiting stage left. As the audience disperses – it's hard to envisage an encore – we'll remain in our seats and keep our heads down, so as not to be recognized. But it seems that we needn't have worried: everyone has taken literally Cage's instruction that whatever happens within those four-and-half minutes should be understood as art. The people filing past are no more perturbed by the guard's speech than had it been delivered during a play which has now finished. Which, in a manner of speaking, it was.

'4'33"' is a provocation. It asks us to think again about what and who we listen to, what we attend to and what we choose to dignify as art. In a conversation with Cage about how he used live radios in musical arrangements such as 'Water Walk', the composer Morton Feldman joked that 'you've got to turn off the radio if you want to be a great artist'. He's making fun of the romantic notion that artists must cut themselves off from the world. While this embrace of the everyday is often taken as exemplary of art's drift into obscurantism it is, in its best examples, a democratic principle (and little different from, for example, Béla Bartók incorporating folk music into his compositions). '4'33"' does not bask in its own strangeness but reminds us that art is not special: it happens all the time and every day, on the street and in people's houses. That the important thing is to keep your ears and your eyes open, and always to pay attention to what you see and hear.

You can decide to treat as art whatsoever you choose. There is no categorical difference between a canvas by Willem de Kooning and the finger painting by your three-year-old that you have pinned by letter magnet to your fridge. This isn't to say that there is no qualitative difference. To illustrate the point, let me show you a sketch I made in my notebook a few days ago. As context, I should say that it was very hot at the time and that I was losing my mind for reasons not unrelated to the woman you heard singing earlier, who has been interfering with my attempts to organize this museum. The drawing is art but it is also, and I cannot stress this enough, very bad art.

If you were to send me your kid's drawing I would be happy to confirm two things: first, it is art. In its rendering of a yellow sun over a house it presents an ideal of domestic and familial life that is consistent with a set of ideological principles and is revealing of Little Jane's psychological state. Second, it is bad art. I could

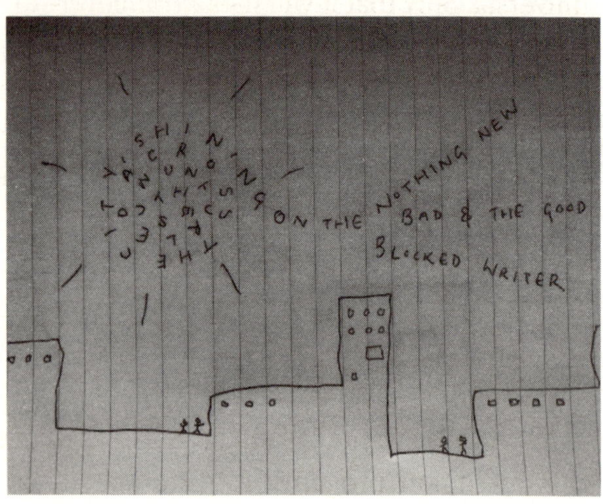

cite its compositional naivety, its appalling insensitivity to the material properties of paint, ignorance of recent theoretical developments in the medium and so on.

Among the things that distinguish a good work of art from a bad one is the quality of its craftsmanship (with the proviso that ideas as much as materials are crafted), its engagement with narratives beyond itself (whether the history of art or society), and the breadth of its appeal (which isn't to say that it needs to be universal, only that it will mean something to a community of people). By these and most other metrics a figurative painting by Rose Wylie or Nicole Eisenman – let's take the latter's *Achilles Heel* (2014), which depicts men sculpting the wax that pours from a bar room's taps – is unarguably better than your darling child's. That doesn't mean you have to prefer it, or that you should reorganize your fridge door accordingly.

No one else wants to look at drawings by me or your infant progeny, so galleries and art history were invented to make sure that they don't waste their time. This is, broadly speaking, a good thing: when you walk into the Museum of Modern Art (MoMA) in New York, you have it on good authority that what you're about to look at is worth looking at, which inclines you to invest time in working out why. But as the recent refurbishment of that institution acknowledged, the stories that a museum tells are – like the meaning of that aforementioned Velázquez – subjective, relational and revealing.

The story that MoMA's founding director Alfred H. Barr chose to tell was one in which modernism was not a break from the European history of art but a continuation of it. It's a familiar story, as in the following (unfairly oversimplified) summary of his 'torpedo model' for art's historical progress: beginning with a series of innovations in France (Gustave Courbet, Édouard Manet, Paul Cézanne) in the second half of the nineteenth century, modern art was taken up across Europe (Edvard

Munch, Gustav Klimt, Giorgio de Chirico), branched out in different ways in the years after the First World War (Otto Dix, Piet Mondrian, Salvador Dalí) and, after the destruction of Europe in the Second, moved to New York, where a new school (Willem de Kooning, Jackson Pollock, Mark Rothko) gave way to Pop (Jasper Johns, Robert Rauschenberg,

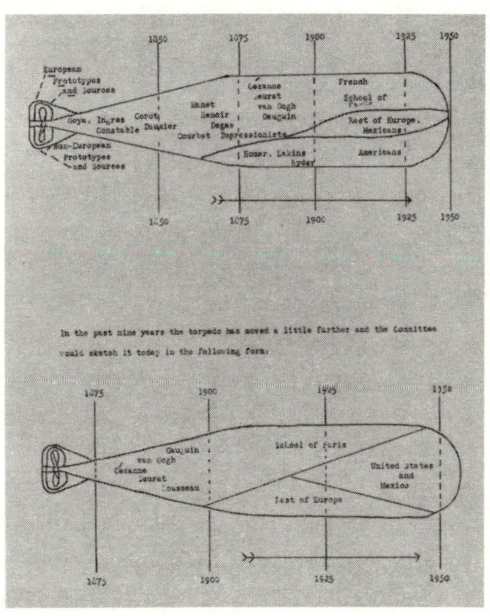

Andy Warhol) and provided the bridge to contemporary art, which took over in the late 1960s.

The United States is positioned as the natural inheritor of white European culture, an historical narrative that prevailed from the mid-twentieth century and is now under challenge from numerous different positions. Just for a start, look at the names in the above pantheon, consider how intricately they are linked by friendship and city of residence, note the absence of women and artists of colour, and consider that this monoculturalism is not an accurate reflection of who was making the most important work but of who was making the decisions about what qualified as the most important work. Even the most qualified experts have an imperfect record of predicting what will endure, and how future societies will think of themselves.

When MoMA reopened after a major refurbishment in 2019, the collection had been rehung to emphasize a much more complex version of the way that modern art and modern society had evolved. Which is to say that the contribution of non-western, non-male and non-white artists to the culture we live in was better represented. As the museum's director Glenn D. Lowry acknowledged, the artforms developed by different communities in response to a changing world 'talked to each other. They weren't independent and isolated conversations'. The museum was reordered to foreground this idea of 'conversation' by showing, for example, how artists in Brazil in the 1960s were responding to recent developments in European art and vice versa. Or that Faith Ringgold's polemical 1967 painting *American People Series #20: Die* can be understood as in 'conversation' with Picasso's *Les Demoiselles d'Avignon* (1907).

The inescapable condition of contemporary art is that it takes place in a world which has been comprehensively globalized, in which we are aware that there is no single, universal and linear tradition but instead an ongoing dialogue between cultures. A world in which we have instant access to text and images from any time in recorded history via the internet, in which the present and the past are more than ever interlinked. Reading art in the twenty-first century is in large part about drawing links between the products of those different cultures, cherishing the familiar and learning about the strange, considering why an image or a story matters to us and what it might mean to others. In light of which, it's worth considering who is making those connections and whether you should trust the story they are trying to tell you. Even when it's me.

Third Floor

I'm worried that the security guard might have posted cronies at the auditorium's exits. Let's walk instead to the front and sneak through a crack by the side of the stage into the wings. Oh, look at all these actors in costumes ...

grizzly bears and astronauts, a whole posse of Snow Whites ... but we don't have time to stay for the next performance. We'll take the service lift, if we can squeeze in next to this woman wearing an electric dress made out of fluorescent strip lights.

The walls of the first gallery on the third floor are covered with brightly coloured throws, fabrics and rugs in a dazzling array of sharp geometric patterns; the floor is crisscrossed with long glass vitrines in which are displayed scraps of cloth, drawings and pattern books. We're going to have to rush through this display of Anni Albers's oeuvre – our time is short – but I wanted to have this twentieth-century great in the museum not only because I have always hankered after one of her works (there's no shame, sometimes, in judging art by the simplest metric: would I want it in my house?) but also because her career illustrates how restrictive the classifications and hierarchies of "high" art can sometimes be, how that reflects on the society that enforces them, and why so much of the art to come after Albers – which is to say, contemporary art – is suspicious of them.

As a young woman growing up between the wars in Germany, Albers was forced into weaving because it was the only workshop open to women at the otherwise famously progressive Bauhaus. So she took the radical experiments in abstraction that were being pioneered at the art school and applied them to rugs, fabrics, room dividers, jewellery and wall hangings. Her work thus gives the lie to a number of enduring prejudices: that art and design should be kept separate; that weaving and other 'women's work' is not art; that industrial processes are not artistic; that fashion isn't art; that women can't be artists, and so on. She was not alone – in 1913, for example, the Bloomsbury Group established the Omega Workshops and Coco Chanel opened her first boutique in Deauville – but I focus on Albers because she takes inspiration from such varied sources and connects them in startling ways.

She also recognized that women were not the only constituency to have been unfairly excluded from the canonical history of art. Displayed here – in conversation with Albers's work – are Wari fabrics woven in the coastal area of what is now Peru over a thousand years ago. When I first came across these ancient textiles I was taken aback by how closely their abstract patterns – ziggurats and labyrinths against red and ochre backgrounds – resemble those on the threadbare rugs in my friends' houses. This is in large part due to Albers' celebration of Andean weaving in her work and writing. That designs serving symbolic purposes in a distant culture now furnish the domestic spaces of European consumers illustrates how the past is refracted through the lens of the present, and how notions of what 'belongs' to a culture have been complicated by globalization and exchange.

Not only does Albers's work undermine artificial separations between modern and pre-modern design, it calls into question what it means to classify objects as art. Andean textiles have traditionally been defined in the West as 'artefacts' and relegated to museums of anthropology, which might lead us to ask why an eighth-century Andean shroud is defined as craft, but a fourteenth-century European funerary monument is art. The application of the word – which is to say, its naming – in these cases reinforces a power dynamic: objects historically fabricated by women or non-European subjects must be other than (meaning inferior to) art. This hierarchy of value has not, notably, prevented western nations from refusing to return to the country of their origin heritage objects looted during the colonial era.

You might be wondering what Albers' mid-century modernism has to do with the more outré things you see in museums these days. But the breakdown in the old divisions between what is art and what is not art – and increased awareness that such distinctions have historically been used to exclude minorities – is at the root of the movement across forms, styles and media that is characteristic of so much art being produced today. Artists including Kader Attia – who uses sculptures, installations, collages, videos and photographs to critique how western societies represent and engage with other cultures – and curators including Anselm Franke at Berlin's Haus der Kulteren der Welt – where sprawling exhibitions are generated by years of research and tackle issues from colonialism to Cold War propaganda – have recently taken this category crisis as a means of widening the remit of what art, artists and institutions can do.

What distinguishes art from the academic disciplines from which it takes cues – whether philosophy, ethnography or sociology – is that it acts on the senses. This recourse to a field of human experience outside reason and beyond language is to art's great advantage, because it legislates against the rehearsal of arguments that seem to their proponents self-evident. We might return to Susan Sontag and Iris Murdoch's demand that we take into consideration the complications of feeling. Sometimes you can't help being attracted to something even though you find it repellent in principle, or vice versa. This ambiguity can encode the kind of complexity that means art resists instrumentalization as propaganda. Art, to put it more simply, can change how you think.

Third Floor (West Wing)

For an example of what I mean, let's go to the bridge that connects the museum to its new west wing (I may have forgotten to mention that we were in the east wing). From this elevated walkway we can look down into the elegant courtyard below, in which I've commissioned the French artist Pierre Huyghe to create one of the miniature worlds on which his reputation as a critical darling of the art world rests. A helpful sign on the railings informs us that the building site below is titled *After ALife Ahead* (2017) and is composed of the following materials: 'concrete floor of ice rink, logic game, ammoniac, sand, clay, phreatic water, bacteria, algae, bees, aquarium, black switchable glass, Conus textile, GloFish, incubator, human cancer cells, genetic algorithm, augmented reality, automated ceiling structure, rain'.

Huyghe builds ecosystems. In the past decade he has taken sites including a patch of woodland or an abandoned ice rink and transformed them into biospheres. Beehives, dogs, artificial intelligences, viruses (benign ones, I should add) and various other organic and inorganic materials are organized into a system, according to which the wellbeing of each is dependent on the whole: here, sensors monitor the movement of the bees and adjust the conditions governing the division of cancer cells in a see-through incubator accordingly, which in turn regulates the opening and closing of a vast skylight above us, which has consequences for the bacteria, which in turn fertilize the soil, and so on. Once the artist has set up this feedback loop, he retreats from it.

Why is this art, you ask? Well, why not? I've always been fascinated by Huyghe's experiments because they ask us to look at the world from a radically different perspective, much like Leo Tolstoy's short story 'Kholstomer', written through the eyes of a horse, or Virginia

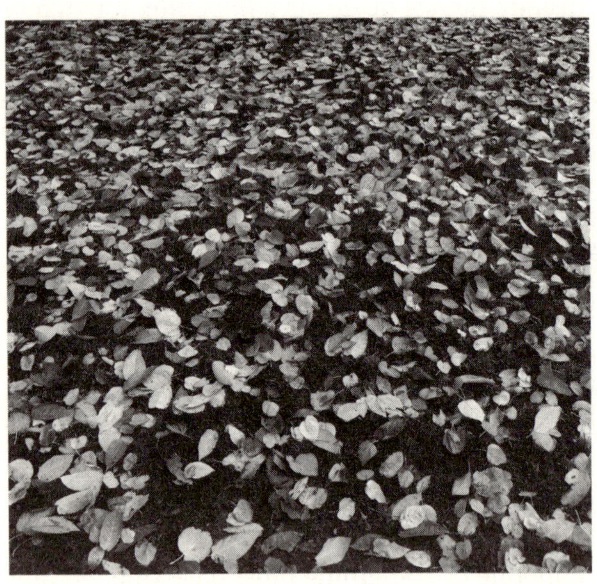

Woolf's 'Flush', which imagines the world as seen by a dog. The scenarios he creates are similarly estranging, forcing the viewer to see how little our species understands of the world that it seems intent on destroying. Which is to say, through it I came to better understand how misguided it is to think that humanity could ever perfectly conceptualize, much less control, nature. No number of popular science articles could have made me more acutely aware of humanity's minor role in an intricate natural system than the experience of wandering through woodland looking for Huyghe's pink-legged dog, although it took a global pandemic and associated economic collapse to really hammer home the point.

The trouble with setting up a self-regulating system to illustrate unintended consequences is, as we should now know better, that it has unintended consequences: you see that black fog that's creeping into the courtyard from an entrance at the south side of the square? Someone or something must have opened one of the basement doors that should never be opened. We better cross to the other side before the gas drifts up on the breeze.

But look, here's my mum. Holding the far end of the bridge, like Horatius.

'Hi, Mum.'

'I've a bone to pick with you.'

'Mum.'

'I hear you've been whingeing about the Rothkos again.'

'Who told you that?'

'A little bird.'

'You mean one of your sisters?'

'I'm asking the questions here. Why are you always badmouthing the Rothkos? You know I like the Rothkos.'

'I didn't badmouth the Rothkos, Mum. The point I was making to my friend here was that everyone's allowed to have an opinion and if something doesn't resonate with you, then it's not necessarily your fault, and you can still recognize its technical excellence and its importance to other people without feeling it necessary to pretend that you experience the same thing, and maybe if we accepted that ...'.

'Don't lie to me. And', she turns to you, 'don't you be minding him. Mark Rothko is much better than all that make-it-up-as-you-go-along stuff he pretends to enjoy, like whatever is going on down there in the courtyard.'

Now back to me, and in a stage whisper.

'Is this a special friend?'

'Mum, no.'

'I'm only asking.'

'Ok Mum, I need to go now. Have you been to see the Pollock?'

'The lights were broken. In a gallery! The staff here, honestly, they're taking advantage of you.'

'This really isn't the time. There are clouds of poisonous gas floating up from the courtyard.'

'Is it those Frenchmen down in the courtyard have let something out?'

'Well not exactly, but I suppose they set in chain a series of complex interdepencies which ...'

'Probably they're looking for drugs, or women.'

'Probably.'

'I'm going to go down there', Mum says, looking at me askance, 'and give them a piece of my mind.'

'OK, love you, Mum. Let's meet outside after you're done.'

Let's keep going.

At the far end of the bridge we move through a sliding door into a room filled with white plinths supporting colourful arrangements of flowers. Let's take a moment to indulge in the simple pleasure of their scent and the combination of natural colours and forms.

You don't need to know much about floristry to deduce that the sprays' bright colours signify celebration, but if you catch that sweet top-note in the fragrance and observe the limpness of the petals, you might gather that these flowers are dying. This installation by Kapwani Kiwanga, who studied anthropology before settling on a career as an artist, is inspired by

the flower arrangements created to mark various African nations' liberation from colonial
rule. The artist researches these bouquets and
boutonnières by watching archive film footage
of the festivals held on each country's independence day, recreates them using the same
indigenous species of flower, and then leaves
them to wilt in the gallery. I imagine that you're
getting from this melancholic spectacle the
same impression of beautiful dreams left to rot
and high hopes fading ...

'Excuse me', says a young woman with an
umbrella in her hand, 'but I couldn't help over-
hearing you talking nonsense.'

'Oh, sorry?'

'This work isn't melancholic, it's angry.'

'Because ...?'

'Because these flowers are left to die. It's
waste.'

'But I think it's a commentary on the way
that the dreams of African nations have with-
ered since the heady days of independence,
because of bad governance and so on ...'

'I think it's because the staff aren't watering the plants.'

'Well, yes, I mean, that's literally true.'

'Which you could say is symbolic of the abandonment of those African nations by the countries that had exploited them, and that still have the power to help them.'

'Um, I guess so.'

'Take Nigeria, represented by these white and pink roses wrapped up in the leaf of a native palm now threatened by extinction. Britain could have done a great deal more after independence to create the conditions in which it might be possible for the new country to flourish. Instead the British government walked away and then, when their ex-colonial subjects came to Britain, they were treated as second-class citizens. This installation is like an allegory for that abandonment. The people who created the problem in the first place stand by, holding up their hands.'

'Is that what you think the artist intended, though?'

'Does it matter?'

'No, I suppose it doesn't.'

'Who are you anyway.'

'I'm the director.'

'You should tell the staff to water the plants.'

'No one listens to me. Anyway, wouldn't that upset your metaphor?'

'They're cut flowers, they need watering. They shouldn't be allowed to die. The intentions of the artist do not dictate the meaning, which can be changed by the interpretation of the viewer. Isn't that the kind of thing you write in your texts?'

'Um ...'

She gives me a polite nod and returns her attention to the flowers. 'I don't want to get involved', she continues, 'I think it's a good work of art. But I hope the invigilators will put their consciences above their instructions.'

Let's hope the imaginary invigilators remember who is paying their imaginary wages. Moving through to the next room, we are confronted by a ten-metre-wide abstract painting resembling a quilted patchwork of red, mauve and turquoise fields swirling around a scattering of black circles. Titled *Ngurrara II*, the painting is a collaboration between artists from the Walmajarri, Wangkajunga, Mangala and Juwaliny communities in northwest Australia, and was created for an unusual reason: to resolve a territorial dispute with the federal government.

In 1997, these interconnected Aboriginal peoples were collectively pursuing official recognition of their status as title holders of a vast stretch of land in northwest Australia, on the principle that their claim preceded and thus superseded that of European settlers. But the claimants faced the problem of how to make their case in a legal tribunal – an issue compounded by indigenous laws requiring that members of a tribe are entitled to speak only of their own land and to disclose only so much of its history to outsiders. Their solution was to create a painting, as the curator Adrian Lahoud explained when he exhibited it in the 2019

Sharjah Architecture Triennial. The first mark on the canvas was laid down by the artist Jimmy Pike, who traced the line of a stock route that runs through the territories. From this, the other artists were able to orient themselves, to mark out their respective lands, and then to paint onto it the dark circles that represent watering holes familiar to hundreds of generations.

When called to testify to the Australian Native Title Tribunal, the communities' representatives rolled the painting out onto the floor of the courtroom and stood on the section marking out their country to make their case (an artist from the Great Sandy Desert region, for example, performed the snake dreaming dance). The painting is a map, but not in the conventional western sense of an objective and to-scale representation of the physical landscape (although the supposed objectivity of maps is, of course, another issue). It is a work of art in that it makes legible the systems of knowledge and shared histories of the societies that inhabit the land, much like a Dutch land-scape painting or a mural by Diego Rivera.

This painting is a map, a record, a performance, a history, an indictment of oppression and a claim to fair recognition and a means of speaking across the gulf separating one system of thought from another. The Federal Court found in favour of the petition. Let's keep going.

Fourth Floor

At the top of the stairs we enter an austere white space dominated by a monumental abstract painting that bears some superficial resemblance to *Ngurrara II*. A dense weave of entangled red, yellow, green, white and orange threads is divided by nine thicker, branching and roughly vertical columns of blue paint that read like the measures in musical notation. Even from a distance the painting communicates a sense of tightly organized chaos but, as we go to inspect its surface more

closely, we are plunged into darkness. This is what mum was complaining about. Don't worry, just count to ten ... the lights come on again. Let's take this chance to observe the room in which we're standing: a cube composed of four white walls lit by spot lamps clamped to steel tracks running across the high ceiling, a poured concrete floor painted an elegant light grey.

This neutral design has some obvious things to recommend it: removing any competing visual noise from a gallery is like soundproofing a concert hall. But it has other effects. If you have been to one of the commercial galleries in west London that sell the expensive work – one you have to buzz to enter before receiving a suspicious look from Inigo on reception – you'll know that this minimalist design is intimidating … the lights go off, and we're back in darkness, I'll carry on … Anyway, it wasn't always such. While works of art were until the early twentieth century typically displayed in 'period rooms' furnished to match the era of their creation, the modernist 'white cube' implies some transcendent realm outside time and space, and confers a sense of specialness on paintings that is to the advantage of those who would sell them. Also, for that matter, museums that would position themselves as the inheritors of cathedrals as spaces in which the public can encounter the divine. The product, as they say, is the atmosphere.

The lights come on again. I might as well tell you that the painting in front of us is Jackson Pollock's *Number 11* (1952), popularly known as *Blue Poles*. Smudged footprints around its edges reveal how the artist (or artists, given that fellow painters Tony Smith and Barnett Newman are sometimes cited as collaborators) laid the canvas on the floor and then poured, smeared, slathered, flung, squeezed and dripped paint onto it. Yet the patterns that emerge from the melee inspire in me a remarkable sense of calm. I find this painting, if you'll forgive the lazy shorthand, extremely beautiful.

And yet I have mixed feelings about it. I don't like the macho mythology that surrounds Pollock (not to mention that many say his lesser-known partner Lee Krasner was the better painter), nor that the artist advised his audience to 'look passively and try to receive what the painting has to offer', as if he were delivering sermons from the mountaintop. I don't like the fact that he is among the painters championed by the art historian Clement

Greenberg to further his theory that the ultimate goal of art is that each form – painting, literature or music – should be reduced to its 'viable essence'. Which is to say that each discipline will gradually insulate itself from the corrupting influence of the others, and from the world in which it is made: painting will only engage with the history of painting, music with the history of music. I'm not saying this isn't an attractive idea, nor am I saying that it is an illegitimate position. I'm just saying I don't agree that art should be fenced off from the world.

The blinking light is not a problem with the wiring, incidentally, but Martin Creed's notorious work of conceptual art *Work No. 227: The lights going on and off*. The flickering light exists to contradict the sublime white decor and remind you, like the dripping tap that stops you from drifting into blissful dreams, that a museum is a constructed environment supported by real-world infrastructures. And the generation of the electricity coursing through the bulb that illuminates Pollock's work is contributing in some small way to the end of the world.

It is also worth recalling that Pollock's enduring fame is at least partly attributable to the CIA. During the Cold War, the 'freedom' of Abstract Expressionism served as a useful analogy for the 'freedom' of American society, and so the CIA funded exhibitions in Europe to win the hearts and minds of the continent's culture-worshipping pinkos. It's not that Pollock's work can't be appreciated as a purely formal arrangement of colours and shapes, or that to do so is necessarily to succumb to the propaganda of American imperialism. But I am always suspicious of art that aspires to some immaculate truth.

I've included Pollock here because he illustrates a point: you can like a work of art at the same time that you distrust it. The school of German painters that came of age in the 1960s were among those to react against their modernist predecessors. They were also, unsurprisingly, determined to resist the co-op-tion of art for political purposes. In the next, much smaller room is a suite of fifteen paint-ings made in 1988 by Gerhard Richter. These ghostly black-and-white images are modelled on photographs of three members of the leftist terrorist organization Red Army Faction found dead in their prison cells eleven years earlier. Richter was born under the Third Reich and grew up in East Germany before moving to the West. At once photorealistic and (like photo-graphs) blurred, these paintings capture his ambivalence towards totalizing systems of truth.

That Richter's greatest paintings are ambiguous doesn't stop his work from selling for vast amounts of money, of course, any more than Pollock's drinking problem has obstructed his own posthumous market. When *Blue Poles* was purchased by the National Gallery of Australia for AS$1.3 million (£700,000) in 1973, it caused a national uproar (the front page of the *Sydney Herald* dismissed it as the product of 'barefoot drunks'). If the outlay seemed extortionate then, it looks like a bargain now: when the painting was loaned to an exhibition at London's Royal Academy in 2017, it was reported to have an insurance value of AS$350 million (£190 million). Putting aside the rampant inflation, the central issue remains the same: is it ethical that an arrangement of oil paint on canvas should be worth that much money? We don't have anything like enough time to go into this, so I'll give you the simple answer: no. However much I like looking at *Blue Poles*, I would happily set fire to it if even a fraction of the insurance money was used to fund programmes encouraging young children to take up the practice of art. I have never been convinced by any argument to the contrary.

On the subject of educating young people, I'm intrigued by the teenager standing in front of the Richters. A wiry sulk in drainpipe jeans and scruffy shoes. As I'm always telling people, the young are the future of this museum. The new generation will inherit and reshape the culture in their own image. The future belongs to them, you know? So let's say hello, see what he can bring to the conversation (because, as I've been saying, it's all about empowering people to join the conversation).

'Hi there! What's your name?'

He returns a moody kind of a look. Unplugs an earphone.

'Ben.'

'Are you enjoying the exhibition?'

'No.'

'Okay – all feedback is good and useful. Why aren't you enjoying it?'

'I've been in here for ages and all I've seen are some bin bags, a crappy pair of glasses, a roomful of singing hippies and a broken light that gave me a headache.'

'You know, Ben, I actually think there was a bit more going on than that summary acknowl-edges. But your opinion is respected here. And it's really important to this museum that differ-ent life views are represented and even that they can enter into a kind of productive tension and conflict, so it's all good! What is it that you *do* like?'

He shrugs. 'I saw this Damien Hirst recently and thought that was good.'

'Well this is interesting. But *why* do you like Damien Hirst?'

'Because he makes work about death and money instead of pretending that art is about accessing some bullshit spiritual place, like yoga or mass, or that it has some meaningful political impact beyond the circle of self-satisfied property owners who go to art openings or the one-percenters who buy it. And he looks like he's having fun. And because people like you probably don't like him, which makes me like him.'

'Cool. But you don't think his work is maybe a bit ... shit?'

'You're a bit shit.'

'Well that's not a very generous way of expressing an opinion, is it Ben? It doesn't really open up the discourse. And you know, the point of having these conflicts between life views is that we can come to a place where there's no resolution – that's what a clever German man named Adorno called a negative dialectic! – and where different positions contribute to a dynamic system but are not resolved into a single, authoritative "truth" about what's good or bad.'

'Like the one you're delivering, right now?'

'Well, actually ...'

'Because', he interrupts, 'it seems like you're saying that I'm wrong but using noncommittal formulations to do it, so that you can feel at the same time that you're right and that you're not dictating to people that you're right? And whoever said self-expression had to be gener- ous? And maybe I don't want to join your conversation?'

He pops his earphone back in and walks away.

Perhaps he's got a point. About the stuff we've seen so far, I mean. I think we're done with this floor now. I need to rehang it. I should have installed some videoworks by Apichatpong Weerasethakul or Korakrit Arunanondchai instead. Sorry. Let's go back to one of the communal areas beside the stairwell, get a coffee and regroup. I want to tell you a little bit about one of my heroes.

'The In-Between'

Whenever the French novelist and occasional art critic J. K. Huysmans was commissioned by a Parisian magazine to review the annual Salon, he would take the reader on an entertainingly bitchy tour of the world's most prestigious exhibition. Walking around the Académie des Beaux-Arts, he disdained the official culture of kitschy mythological paintings, 'miraculously banal' panoramas and 'deplorably sentimental' portraiture showcased in 1879 ('I hate with all my might the majority of paintings exhibited'); 1880 ('mediocrity is in operation this year, more furiously than ever'); 1881 ('even more laughable than those of previous years'); and 1882 ('I will restrict myself to citing a few works that cannot be confused with the worm-eaten fruits of this bargain basement').

Having failed to find much of worth in the 1880 Salon, the organizers having rejected most of the Impressionist and post-Impressionist painters that the writer admired, Huysmans steps out into the street. There he finds Jules Chéret's posters for the city's cabarets plastered to the railings, and pronounces them to be of greater artistic value than anything in the exhibition:

> I can only counsel people sickened ... by this cheap and insulting display of prints and paintings to cleanse their eyes by directing them outdoors ... where shine the astonishing fantasies of Chéret. There is a thousand times more talent in the smallest of these posters than in the majority of the paintings that I have had the sad opportunity to review.

This might sound like hyperbole – a sensationalist journalist looking for a headline – but history has proved him right. The majority of the artists feted by the establishment at the time have retreated into relative obscurity (Édouard Debat-Ponsan), aged badly (Antoine Vollon) or been overtaken (Jules Bastien-Lepage) by their more radical peers, while the advertisements for the Folies Bergère remain extraordinarily fresh. Drawing on Rococo painting and Japanese printmakers such as Hokusai, Chéret's lithographs went on to inspire artists including Georges Seurat (whose pointillism is itself a precursor of Roy Lichtenstein and Sigmar Polke's imitation of printing dots in their work). It seems, with the benefit of hindsight, that any Belle Époque Parisian with eyes to see should have been able to spot that these advertisements were infinitely more interesting than the lifeless pastoral idylls and gloopy portraits inside the real and figurative Academy.

To develop the point that the market is rarely a good measure of what will be remembered, I was flirting with the idea of installing in my museum a miniature version of one of the contemporary art fairs that are today's equivalents of the Salon. And then pouring scorn on the appalling works of art contained within and the stupidity of their collectors. But those bin bag sculptures at the entrance are there to remind me not to surrender to cynicism, so I thought it better to follow the Frenchman's example by seeking beauty in the streets. Have you finished your coffee? That fire escape is a shortcut down to the street below. What? Of course the alarm won't go off if you open it, I'm making this museum up as I go along. Just push at the metal bar ...

OK, so the alarm went off. Big deal. Bang the door shut and let's hurry down the staircase that zigzags the outside of the building. If we move quickly we can get out of sight before the security guard works out what's going on.

Notice anything unusual about the street, by the way? All these afro-haired roller-skaters zipping along the pavement? The hip-hop blaring from a ghetto blaster carried on the shoulder of a young woman wearing glasses with tinted lenses and oversized round frames? That bare-chested man in a leather waistcoat leaning against a graffiti-strewn wall? That picturesque burst of hot steam from an uncovered manhole? And, wow, doesn't that look a lot like Grace Jones, walking down the street arm-in-arm with Grandmaster Flash and Andy Warhol?

We're in downtown New York circa 1983! Or rather, we're in my thinly researched imaginary version of New York circa 1983. For my most ambitious exhibition space, I've taken over a street outside the museum and choreographed a vast performance based on my vague idea of what downtown New York might have looked like at that time. The people on these streets are all actors, paid to remain strictly in character for the duration of this chapter.

On the street beside the bottom rung of the ladder is a lamppost, onto which a polemical poem has been sloppily plastered. On the wall

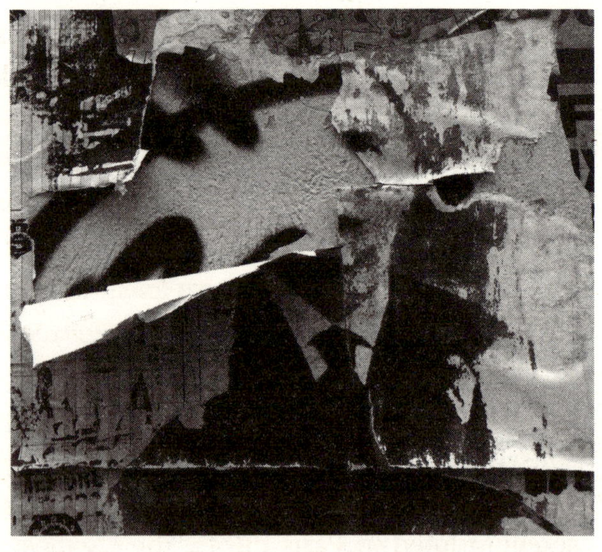

across the pavement is spray-painted the phrase 'SAMO@ AS AN ALTERNATIVE TO PLASTIC FOOD STANDS', which if it still existed would be on the market as an early work by Jean-Michel Basquiat (or protected by a sheet of Perspex, like Banksy's tribute to the artist in the underpass beside London's Barbican Art Gallery). Further down the road there's a mural by the graffiti artist Lady Pink, while an empty billboard hoarding above a metro station is decorated by a fluent, ideogrammatic chalk drawing by Keith Haring of two dancing men.

These documents of a storied period in New York's cultural history, in which these and other artists worked on the streets of a city in crisis, are now conserved in museums and traded in auction houses. The transformation of even explicitly anti-capitalist statements into tradable commodities is among the more dispiriting consequences of expanding the field of art. I was depressed recently to learn that a poster screen-printed in Paris during the May 1968 uprisings, and declaring that 'Beauty is in the Street', had sold at auction in 2018 for €3,800.

Artists are not unaware of this absurdity. On the corner, a man is selling snowballs of various sizes to pedestrians; ahead of us, another is dragging himself belly-down along the sidewalk with a skateboard strapped to his back. The former is the artist David Hammons and the latter Pope.L, who has been crawling through the streets of New York since the late 1970s in protest at the city's inequalities. The spectacle of a black man pulling himself up Broadway draws attention to the number of people living on the streets, and the fact that these people should not, as the artist puts it, be treated quite so much 'like pieces of shit'. Both of these performances could be read as vicious satires against a society in which works of art generate vast profits for those prepared to play the market while their fellow citizens remain without food or shelter.

But look, there's the security guard, asking David Hammons whether he has a licensed permit to sell snowballs. Before he spots us, let's slip quietly down this alleyway lined with overflowing trash cans and animatronic rats (health and safety dictated that I wasn't able to import real ones) and reach a black metal door at its dead end. It takes us into a passageway that leads back to the main building.

I'll use this short journey to explain that in the real world, I'm sat at a desk, adorned with a single potted plant and a bottle of Alfa beer, in a flat with a view over Athens. This morning I went for a walk around the neighbourhood in which I'm staying, which is famous for the anarchist and squatting subcultures expressed in the graffiti that cover every available inch of wall space. I was hoping to find some contemporary equivalent to the posters that Huysmans celebrated or the drawings by Haring that decorated New York's metro carriages, and use it to illustrate my now laboured point about visual culture not being confined to museums. Among the antifa slogans and dire threats to Airbnb customers (pointedly in English) I was drawn to a doodle, perhaps because I'd recently seen *Orphée* at one of Athens's rooftop cinemas and it reminded me of Jean Cocteau's fluent line drawings. So I took a picture on my phone.

It was only when I backed away that I noticed that the wall adjoined a recessed shop front: you can just make it out at the image's right edge. In this narrow alcove a man lay sleeping on a thin mattress, surrounded by bundles that

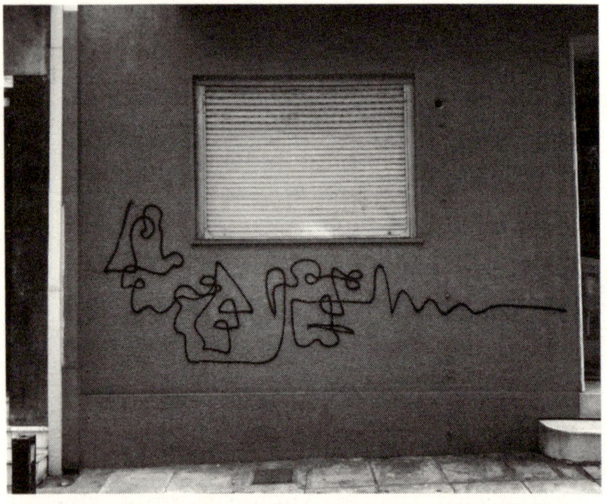

he had hoisted up from the floor on makeshift string pulleys.

I felt ashamed: a tourist taking snaps of the 'authentic' Athens while ignoring the man who slept rough. You can see how I unconsciously framed the photograph, placing the drawing at the centre of the white wall and cropping out anything extraneous to it. And how, in doing so, I cut out of the picture the man suffering from the effects of the social and economic crises that critics like me are liable to pontificate upon in discussions of contemporary Greek art. In looking for art that might tell me about the city, I had made myself blind to its realities.

It's important when looking at any image – whether a painting or an Instagram post – to consider what the taker has left out of the frame. What is the influencer choosing not to include in her picture diary from a Saudi Arabian music festival? Why has this rediscovered picture of a politician meeting some unsavoury character twenty years ago been cropped to remove the surroundings? Sometimes it's possible to find a clue that inadvertently disrupts the constructed truth of the image, like that offered by the fabric in the corner of the above photograph. How we frame art – where we place the borders that separate it from the world – is one way of excluding from our vision of the world anything that challenges how we are conditioned to see it.

Fifth Floor

Emerging from the steep passage onto the museum's fifth floor, we are greeted by a crowd of people carrying banners, handing out pamphlets and waving placards. These protesters have been occupying this part of the museum ever since I started thinking about it. I'll leave it to your imagination to decide the issue that has provoked them to action, but here are some options: the business dealings of the museum's board members; its sponsorship by companies made rich through fossil fuel extraction; the museum's unconscious but increasingly apparent bias towards European and American artists; its contribution to the gentrification of the neighbourhood in which it is stationed ... I'm sure you won't struggle to come up with something.

Museums are among the most visited tourist attractions in the world's major cities and, whether funded by the state or through private

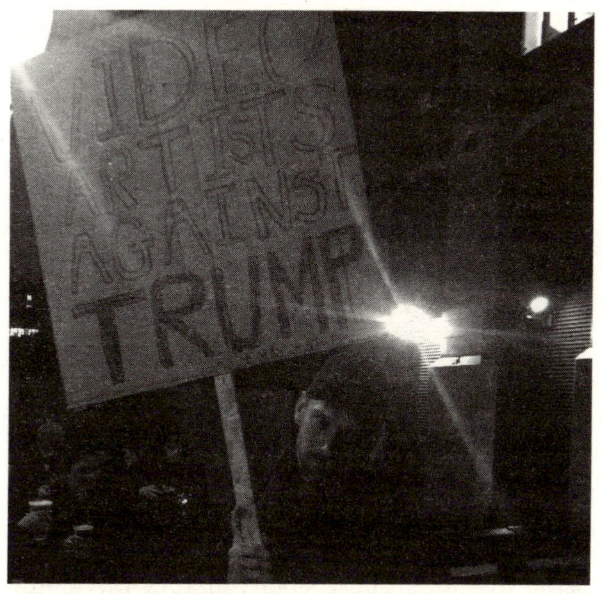

wealth, whether focusing on the nation's past or looking to the outside world, they tell you something about the places in which they are stationed. Which makes them ideal platforms for expressions of dissent and debate. Moving through the protesters we enter a blacked-out gallery, at the centre of which is a plain wooden bench. On the facing wall is a slideshow of photographs by Nan Goldin depicting the drag queens, punks and junkies with whom she hung out in the late 1970s and 1980s, soundtracked by the Velvet Underground and Charles Aznavour. Taking its title from a song in Bertolt Brecht and Kurt Weill's 'The Threepenny Opera' (1928), Goldin's *The Ballad of Sexual Dependency* (1986) took on new meaning when she launched her own personal campaign against those she held responsible for the opioid epidemic now sweeping the United States.

Goldin became dependent on the highly addictive painkiller OxyContin after being prescribed it for tendonitis in her wrist. When the prescription ran out, she moved – like tens of thousands of others – onto street drugs (47,000 people died in the United States from opioid overdoses in 2017). It took her four years to kick the habit, at which point she discovered that the pharmaceutical company responsible for manufacturing and aggressively marketing OxyContin was owned by a family who donate millions of pounds to museums each year. She established an advocacy group and staged protests around the world, threatening to withdraw her work from exhibitions at institutions that accepted 'dirty money' from the Sackler family. The campaign was successful, and in 2019 the Louvre, the National Gallery in London and the Metropolitan Museum in New York, among others, announced that they would not take donations from the Sackler Trust and Foundation. A critically acclaimed show of Goldin's work at Marian Goodman Gallery in London late in the same year included documentation of these protests alongside photographs of friends of the artist who had fallen victim to addiction, transforming her moral crusade into art. Her actions have dramatically changed the cultural landscape: do all art organizations now have a responsibility to make sure that their funding is not tainted by association?

Individual works of art can also serve as lightning rods for debates about how society understands itself, as the first work in the following gallery illustrates. Our view is obscured by a man wearing a T-shirt with the slogan 'Black Death Spectacle' on its back. If we peer around him, we see a painting of a black boy's body in an open coffin. His face, which occupies the left half of the picture, is rendered in hashed brushstrokes that reduce his features to a mussed abstraction. Dana Schutz's *Open Casket* (2016) depicts the mutilated corpse of Emmett Till, a fourteen-year-old boy lynched in 1955 for having looked a white woman in the eye, as it was captured in a photograph that became a touchstone for the Civil Rights movement. When her painting was included in the 2017 Whitney Biennial in New York – a prestigious survey exhibition of American art – it was accused of sensationalizing racist violence. Hence this man's silent protest.

The objection is that this work by a white woman from New Zealand transforms one of the most potent images in the history of racial struggle in the United States into titillation for a presumptively white audience. Or, as an open letter by the artist and writer Hannah Black put it, 'it is not acceptable for a white person to transmute Black suffering into profit and fun'. The 'profit' alludes to the likely increase in the artist's market value that comes from being included in such a significant exhibition, the 'fun' presumes that the general public necessarily treats paintings as light entertainment. (Whether or not the artist intended to condemn the history of American racism was beside the point.) Is the issue with this painting that an artist should never attempt to represent experiences beyond her own, or is it more subtle: the handling of the paint serving as an unacceptably weak signifier of the very real damage done to this young boy's body?

Past a series of framed photographs by the South African artist Zanele Muholi, a painting by Mickalene Thomas (*Le déjeuner sur l'herbe: les trois femmes noire*, 2010) and a video by Nam June Paik that doesn't really belong here but I couldn't find anywhere else to put, hangs a painting set in a barber's salon. Kerry James Marshall's *De Style* (1993) features three black figures with elaborate hairdos staring out at the viewer, and is one significant work in an oeuvre that has put African American bodies at the centre of a pictorial tradition from which they have traditionally been excluded. Like Thomas, Marshall engages with the history of art in order to change it: *A Portrait of the Artist as a Shadow of His Former Self* (1980) reduces the artist's face to white teeth and eyes against black skin and background. It plays on James Joyce's quasi-autobiographical novel to position this black artist within a canonical tradition even as the caricatured representation signals his exclusion from it, and makes for a productive comparison against ...

But a young woman carrying a placard is approaching.

'Are you the director of this museum?' she demands.

'Um, no?'

'Yes, you are.'

'OK, yes I am.'

'Why did you lie?'

'Well I got in trouble earlier for saying that I *was* the director.'

'No, you were trying to evade a public discussion around the fact that the museum inscribes art histories that are sexist and racist.'

'I really wasn't. No one believes that I'm in charge except you. And, look, if we're talking about the Dana Schutz painting, I didn't put it in here because I like it – I agree with the problems you identify – but rather to encourage people to talk about those problems. Which is what you're doing with this protest, isn't it? I'm wholeheartedly behind you, by the way. This is the kind of messy and incoherent debate that happens in a functioning society.'

'I have a problem', she continues, 'with the way you've installed Kerry James Marshall's work. It's presented as some kind of counterpoint, which is typical of the kind of lazy curatorial decision-making that sees [air quotes] "balance" in a debate as equivalent to proper ethical representation of the issue, like on the news when they [air quotes] "balance" a discussion on climate change by setting a scientist against some incel who thinks climate change is a conspiracy orchestrated by George Soros. Besides which, the Kerry James Marshall painting is a much more accomplished painting on every level, so that kind of false equivalence is offensive.'

'I see your point, and actually that's kind of what I was just saying, but ...'

'Good. What's up with the Gauguin?'

Ah, we missed this. Paul Gauguin's *Sacred Spring, Sweet Dreams (Nave nave moe)* (1894) is hanging in one of the rooms in the basement galleries.

'Look, I'll be honest', I reply. 'I loved Gauguin's paintings when I was a teenager. The hazy tones, the easy rhythms, the rough harmonies. I can see now that his paintings of Polynesian women are misogynist, that they play into exoticizing stereotypes. But I don't necessarily think that means we should hide them away. Thinking again on *Nave nave moe* alerted me to some uncomfortable issues with the ways that western culture teaches young men to look at women from different cultures. Showing the work and talking about it might help men to recognize that.'

'But the presumption is that your visitors are white men like you and that the museum exists for their edification. There's also the problem that by so explicitly politicizing the works of Kerry James Marshall you're making it impossible for the visitor to understand them on their own terms, to see them as engaged with the history of painting. Which is a privilege reserved, it seems, for white artists, who are allowed to be [air quotes] "universal".'

'But I did the flashing light thing for Pollock in the other gallery! I thought that was …'

'Besides which', she continues, 'it's not enough to [air quotes] "make these works available", you have to change the infrastructure of the institution. You need more diverse curatorial staff, you need research into ways of talking about art that reflect different perspectives and cultures, you need to find more inclusive ways of bringing audiences other than old white people into the museum and, most of all, you must work harder to disentangle the museum from the structures of power. Who is paying for all this? There's no transparency at all.'

'OK, fine. I get it. The thing is, and I don't know if this has been made clear, but this museum is actually an essay. It might be that some of the curatorial decisions only work in a discursive piece of nonfiction rather than in an actual museum, and perhaps not even then. Notwithstanding that, the point I'm trying to make is that art should elicit these kinds of debates and that there is no single resolution or way of reading art. And that art is a conversation, like the one we're having now ...?'

I trail off.

She's looking sideways at me.

'You're saying that all this is in your mind?'

'Well, kind of. See, the whole exercise is a pun on something a Victorian art critic once wrote about the feelings of a great nation being legible in the book of its art. So I thought, why not write a book of art and then ask people to read and interpret it, and in doing so to question whether it is 'great nations' who any longer inscribe themselves into art, or individuals, or communities. And that book of art is also this museum. So we're kind of, umm, in the book?'

She's backing away. In fact, she's going to talk to the invigilator, who is sitting in the corner reading a novel. Now he's pulling out his walkie-talkie. We had better move on again. Look, the grille on this air vent has conveniently been unscrewed. I'm going to create a distraction and, during the commotion, you crawl into the shaft. Just imagine you're in an old spy film for which the screenwriter couldn't think of a more imaginative escape route. I'll follow. Get ready ...

'IS THAT GRETA THUNBERG?!'

Go, go, go!

The Tunnels

Sorry to make you wriggle through the ventilation system that runs through the museum, it was really the only way I could think of to get out of that situation. We can escape by moving towards the distant thump that's reverberating down the shaft. See that flickering red light at the end of the tunnel? Kick your foot through the bars of the grille and we can jump down into a control room.

The cramped space is illuminated by a flashing red strip light and pulses with the beat of a synchronized heartbeat. The walls are covered with documents showing the results of phonocardiogram tests and blood analyses alongside a grid of annotated photographs of a young woman's face. There are medical records and identity cards, and together they form a portrait in words, sounds and images of the Peruvian artist Teresa Burga on a single day in 1972. Burga's native Peru was at the time ruled by

General Juan Velasco Alvarado's military dictatorship and so, by representing herself through medical statistics, she seems to criticize the tendency of authoritarian regimes to depersonalize citizens (specifically its female citizens) by reducing them to data. But you don't need to know this to be caught up in the febrile atmosphere created by the flash and punch of the heartbeat. This heightened awareness of the heart, and the claustrophobia it provokes, strikes at fears that cannot be so easily articulated.

We squeeze into a corridor, past an alcove featuring a sculpture in plaster by Alina Szapocznikow of a five-foot-tall woman with what appears to be an illuminated resin flower petal for a head (*Illuminowana*, 1966–67), through a curtain and into a tiny cinema cavern. At the end of one of the four rows of seats, a man in a trilby hat is sleeping. The bright blue rectangle on the screen suggests that the projector is broken, but after a few seconds you'll notice that the monochrome is flecked by the hairline scratches of imperfections on analogue film. Made in the months before the artist and filmmaker Derek Jarman's death from AIDS-related complications, *Blue* (1993) is an hour-and-a-half of flickering blue frames accompanied by a soundtrack and voice-over which splices an imaginative fiction with details from the artist's own hospital visits. In its combination of social commentary, snatches of poetry and reflections on what it means to occupy a body, this work is, like Burga's, at once witty, polemical and moving.

Like all good art, it is complicated in that its effects are governed by a web of cultural, ethical and historical factors and simple in that it just happens to you. Or as A. R. Ammons put it, 'I have not found the flavor of orange / juice diminished or increased by this or that approach to Heidegger or *Harmonium.*' To articulate what attracts you to someone – the patterns their thought takes, their face when sleeping, the smile over their shoulder, the grace of their posture at the top of a staircase – is to attempt to make sense of the felt experience of love. But the symptoms don't entail the feeling, however brilliantly you anatomize them, and your friend might agree that the object of your affection has unusually elegant shoulder blades without falling in love with them. Speaking of which, and because I've now summoned her into being, I can hear the woman we saw earlier singing. She must be in the next room.

The problem is that I can't get her out of my mind. Thoughts of her have shaped the unreal architecture of this building, the selection of works, the relations between them and the way that I've responded to them. She might even be the reason that I've been making the case that art is a way of understanding not only the society in which you live but the way you feel and what you care about. That we should embrace rather than attempt to transcend our own feelings, experiences and politics when looking at art, and that this might help us to come to terms with how reason and emotion combine to shape our behaviour. Art is not escapism and

museums are not sanctuaries. And now, echo-
ing tinnily through the ventilation shafts, comes
the security guard's whistle. Notwithstanding
what I just said about escapism, we need to get
out of here.

The Burrow

I sink to my knees and with my index finger
trace four lines into the floor. The lines glow
and resolve into the cracks of light at the edges
of a trapdoor. I'll pull the hatch up and together
we can step down the ladder beneath it into a
cluttered and windowless room, seven metres
by six.

The walls are crowded with posters and
Polaroids; a small desk is stacked with post-
cards and papers; bookshelves run along one
wall. On a tatty rug laid out on the otherwise
bare floorboards is a low table carrying a record
player, a potted aspidistra, the catalogue from
a show at Palais de Tokyo in Paris, a postcard of

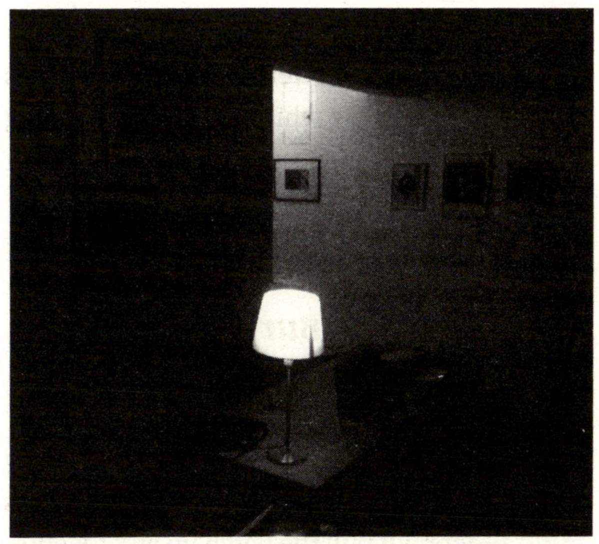

Leonardo's *St Anne* (1503) with its blue mountains, a delicate Korean celadon pot, and a framed potato print. Hanging on the wall to our left is a seascape over which someone has painted a fire-breathing Big Bird. That mournful man in the corner playing an acoustic guitar is the Icelandic artist Ragnar Kjartansson. He's watching a short film on an old television monitor in which a family continue at their lives as the house around them burns to the ground. Francisco de Goya has painted a black land-scape directly onto the ceiling, suspended from which is a clattering projector which beams a silent black-and-white horror movie onto the opposite wall. I'll pull out a shoebox from under the table and peel away the tape that binds the lid to its body. Inside, wrapped in tissue paper, is a narrow hairband composed of latticed strips of bent brown wood. The distinction between canonical masterpieces and objects of sentimental value breaks down in this final room: if things mean what they do to you, then these are the most meaningful things in my life.

They are also the fragments on which the story of a self can be founded. Each carries an association to something – a formative experi-ence, a loved person, a set of values, someone lost – that has shaped the way I act in the world. I think of the pattern connecting these private keepsakes to the wider culture expressed in art as a thread that binds me together. We write ourselves into being by connecting what happens to us, and which belongs to us alone, with the stories told by the communities we identify with. The two exist in dynamic exchange, which is to say a conversation.

I started this essay by asking how we might read the book of contemporary art, and who gets to write it. Unlike John Ruskin, I don't have much faith in great nations or the idea that the lives of their citizens could be condensed into a single authoritative account. Rather than a sacred text, I think of the book of art as an unresolved, disputatious and polyvocal conversation in which we are all engaged.

This essay, on that principle, has failed to provide anything like a concrete definition of what art is today. That was always a red herring, and I'm sorry for having led you on. And it's perhaps late in the day to admit that I don't recognize art as a dead category capable of definition at all, but as the human urge to express our position in relation to a universe electrified by consciousness. We all make art, all of the time, by using memory and imagination to arrange the meagre materials we have to hand into stories that make sense of the mysteries of pain and love. So I hope that this essay might encourage you to write your own story, to build your own museum, even to walk me through it one day. But now it's time to go outside.

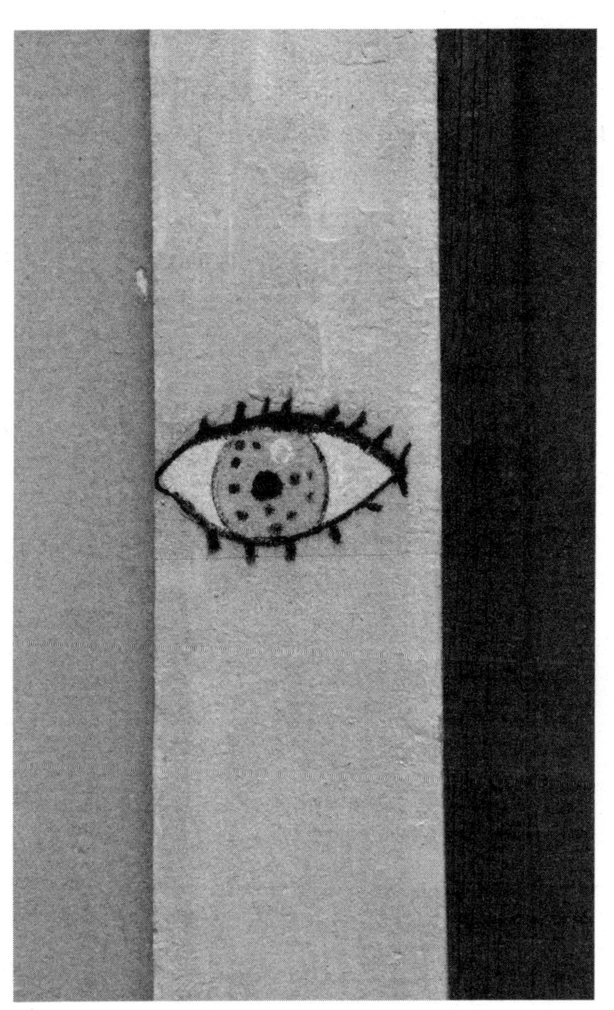

Acknowledgements

I am grateful to Roz Dineen at TLS Books, to Anna Webber for her encouragement, to Maria Dimitrova, Patrick Langley, Jacques Testard and many others for their conversations. To Navine G. Khan Dossos and James Bridle for trusting me with their plants. To Ulya Soley for being a nuisance. Thanks to my mum, with apologies for having so grievously (lovingly!) misrepresented her. To the memory of Luisa de Lancastre.

Special thanks to Lea Bauer, whose photographs are another thread through this book.

Audio guide: List of referenced works

Introduction

The sculpture that so bewilders the narrator is Roger Hiorns' *Untitled* (2011), the materials of which are officially listed as 'military aircraft engine, fire, youth'. The battered hard drives allude to Revital Cohen and Tuur Van Balen's *b/NdAlTaAu* (2015) and the towels were stacked on a shelf on the instruction of Ai Weiwei, who titled his miniature pyramid *Rare Towel* (2015). NB that it was the narrator's first assignment does not necessarily mean it was the author's.

The looping performance of Schubert was staged by Ragnar Kjartansson for the London Contemporary Music Festival in 2017; the virtual reality experiences of the moon were provided by Antony Gormley and Priya

Natarajan's (painstakingly researched but science-museum boring) *Lunatick* (2019) and Laurie Anderson and Hsin-Chien Huang's (hallucinogenic, beautiful) *To the Moon* (2019); the beach opera is a collaboration between Lina Lapelytė, Vaiva Grainytė and Rugilė Barzdžiukaitė which debuted as Lithuania's contribution to the 2019 Venice Biennale, hidden down a backstreet (when I arrived, an invigilator on the door was explaining to a visitor that she had succeeded in finding the Lithuanian Pavilion, to which she replied 'No, I said *Where's Lithuania*'); the Sinhalese lesson was part of Tania Bruguera's *School of Integration* at Manchester Art Museum in the same year; the cyberpunk vision of Silicon Valley is Zach Blas's *Jubilee 2033* (2018), which reimagines Derek Jarman's 1978 new-wave *Jubilee*.

Tate Liverpool presented Rachel Whiteread's sculptures and architectural projects in the exhibition *Shedding Life* (September 1996–January 1997). When discussing, and doing scant justice to, Mark Rothko's work, the sceptical narrator has in mind the Rothko Chapel in Houston, Texas, a 'non-denominational sanctuary' which is nonetheless sanctified by the Latvian-American artist's paintings and scattered with pamphlets about spiritual healing.

Beatriz González's *Interior Decoration* (Decoración de Interiores) (1981) reproduces a glossy magazine photograph of the then-president of Colombia amid glamorous company at a glitzy official function. The use of cheap techniques and materials (silk screening, industrial fabric) to represent the scene critiques his government's hypocrisy and corruption, while its formal resemblance to a screen or curtain suggests the veil of secrecy drawn over the regime's human rights abuses.

The curious double life of Ad Reinhardt as one of the greatest and most austere of the mid-century New York School – most famous for his uncompromising black-on-black paintings – and witty satirist and cartoonist

illustrates that humour is not only no disquali-
fier to seriousness but integral to it.

Like *Hamlet* (1609), Velázquez's enigmatic *Las Meninas* (1656) – in the collection of the Prado in Madrid – endures because it rewards the different interpretations placed upon it by each new generation.

Ground Floor

In addition to the three black bin bags, Andreas Lolis also contributed a trompe-l'oeil duvet and pillow in white marble to the 2019 Venice Biennale: they were laid invitingly out on a park bench, highlighting issues of homelessness in the art world's Disneyland.

The Imaginary Museum's atrium is lit, like the Museum of Modern Art in New York, by Philippe Parreno's glowing marquees; the harlequin-patchwork benches on which people are sitting and talking are works by the late, great Austrian artist Franz West.

In 2016, shortly after the opening of the

recently refurbished San Francisco Museum of Modern Art, two teenagers from San Jose decided to test the credulity of its visitors by placing a pair of spectacles on the ground. They posted pictures of the resulting crowds on Instagram.

Carl Andre's *Equivalent VIII* (1966), popularly known in the UK as *The Bricks*, became notorious when its exhibition at the Tate in 1976 was greeted by the *Daily Mirror* headline 'What a Load of Rubbish'. In terms of works of art that are liable to rub the readers of British tabloid newspapers up the wrong way, it's canonical.

The Tate Modern displays a 1964 replica of Marcel Duchamp's *Fountain* (1917) which started life, of course, as a urinal. If you think about what it means to reproduce and authenticate as a work of art an object that was supposed in the first place to undermine the definition of a work of art in terms of 'originality' and 'authenticity', then you're liable to get your head in a twist. But that's both the point of the work and its reward. Duchamp's work is a little like Samuel Beckett's writing in that, if you can't pick out the loose threads of humour in these logical convolutions, you're liable to get tied up in knots.

First Floor

The revolving door through which you and the narrator escape has been transplanted from *Indiana Jones and the Last Crusade* (1989), unquestionably the artistic high-water mark of that film franchise.

As a painter and critic, the Sumatran artist Sindoedarsono Sudjojono adapted some of the innovations of twentieth-century European painting to the social, political and historical contexts of Indonesia, not to mention its particular light and landscape. Which is to say that his work helps to illustrate how movements evolve differently depending on the conditions under which they are practised. The ceramics thrown and painted by the husband-and-wife Frimkesses combine an obsession with Attic vases with the pop iconography of twentieth-century America.

Tino Sehgal's *This Variation* was performed at the 2012 edition of Documenta, curated by Carolyn Christov-Bakargiev. The German artist Joseph Beuys, whose *7,000 Oak Trees* (1982) adorn the city of Kassel, is famous for his credo that 'Everyone is an artist'. The bullshitting to which the text refers might more generously be described as 'self-mythologizing' and encompasses a fanciful story about having been rehabilitated by kind-hearted Tatar nomads who wrapped him in felt and animal fat after his plane was shot down over Crimea during the Second World War.

Second Floor

The painter Lubaina Himid – a key member of the British Black Arts Movement of the 1980s – became the first black woman to win the Turner Prize in 2017. Since 1991 she has been based in Preston, the city in which my grandparents lived and where I spent stretches of my childhood, and her success has inspired in me a sense of affiliation that also feels fraudulent, in the sense that I don't belong to the community to which her work is often presumed to speak. But there are many ways of connecting with an artist through her biography, and its traces in her work.

The blank projection above the pianist performing John Cage's *4'33"* (1952) is a nod to *Zen for Film* (1965) by an important inheritor of Cage's legacy, the Korean artist and musician Nam June Paik. If you have got this far without watching John Cage's *Water Walk* (1960) on an online video-sharing platform, treat yourself.

The very deliberate placement of Faith Ringgold's sharply politicized and unflinchingly confrontational *American People Series #20: Die* (1967) – which depicts the race riots that scarred US cities in the late 1960s – next to the *Demoiselles,* a treasure of the collection which plays on queasy ideas of primitivism and

African otherness, provoked a great deal of commentary when MoMA reopened, which is to the curators' credit.

Third Floor

The costumed figures backstage are plucked from Mark Wallinger's *Sleeper* (2004), which follows the artist as he wanders through Berlin's deserted Neue Nationalgalerie (Wallinger also created the labyrinthine drawing on this book's cover); a 2017 performance by Manila-based artist Eisa Jocson in Snow White cosplay; Halil Altindere's *Space Refugee* (2017), a tribute to Syrian astronaut and exile Muhammed Ahmed Faris. The young woman in the lift is Atsuko Tanaka, who is modelling her own *Electric Dress* (1965).

The organization of Anni Albers' work in this section, and its juxtaposition with the textiles from South America that inspired it, owes much to the retrospective of her work at Tate Modern in 2018, *Josef Albers in Mexico* at the New York

Guggenheim in the same year, and *Ancient Textiles in the Andes* at the Whitworth in Manchester in 2019.

Third Floor (West Wing)

In its original – i.e. non-imaginary – installation, Pierre Huyghe's *After ALife Ahead* (2017) occupied a disused ice rink in the German town of Münster, which every ten years hosts a massive and much-anticipated sculpture festival named Skulptur Projekte Münster. As in the case of Documenta and Kassel, the town has come to be shaped and in part defined by the sculptures scattered through it.

Another opportunity to remind you that this is the *narrator*'s Irish mother that he meets on the bridge, and that any resemblance to real persons or other real-life entities is purely coincidental.

Kapwani Kiwanga's *Flowers for Africa* is an ongoing project which the artist has described as 'shifting the way one looks' at historical events. Gerhard Richter's series *October 18, 1977* (1988) – in the next gallery – does something similar, asking us to attend to a significant moment in the political history of a nation and leaving judgement upon it to the viewer.

Fourth Floor

I'm indebted here to Adrian Lahoud's essay about *Ngurrura II* (1997) in *ArtReview* (August 2019). Martin Creed's *Work No. 227: The lights going on and off* (2000) will be familiar to anyone who remembers the halcyon days when every announcement of the Turner Prize was greeted by confected fury in the tabloids. The ubiquity of Jackson Pollock's paintings now is a reminder of how art that once incited bafflement soon settles into bourgeois good taste and, ultimately, biscuit-tin kitsch (cf. the Impressionists).

Apichatpong Weerasethakul is a Thai film-maker best known for *Uncle Boonmee Who Can Recall His Past Lives*, winner of the Palme d'Or at Cannes in 2010; Korakrit Arunanondchoi is a hip, hyped and enviably well-connected young Thai video artist.

The In-Between

To prove the point being made here, search online for Jules Chéret's thrilling posters for the Moulin Rouge or the Folies Bergère. Keep the tab open, then search for Édouard Debat-Ponsan, and compare his pictures of pale-faced milkmaids mooning over freshly picked flowers with Chéret's cabaret dancers. Academic art is always inflated at the time of its production because it is approved by the systems from which it emerges. A similarly unflattering comparison could be drawn between any number of two-bit conceptual artists from the 1980s and the graphic design of Peter Saville, and no doubt much of the consensus-clever, prof-pleasing work now emerging from art schools in New York and London will go the same way.

Jean-Michel Basquiat and his school friend Al Diaz started writing cryptic messages around downtown New York in 1978, such as 'SAMO© 4 the SO-CALLED AVANT GARDE' and 'SAMO© AS AN END 2 CONFINING ART TERMS'. Inevitably, Basquiat's witty critiques of the art world's pretensions did not save his work from being traded for vast sums on its market, especially after his myth-enhancing death at the age of twenty-seven. The record is held by an untitled painting of a skull dating from 1982, which sold at Sotheby's New York for the frankly immoral sum of $110.5 million in May 2017.

The poster poem is one of Jenny Holzer's *Inflammatory Essays* (1979-82), cut-up texts of 100 words in 20 lines composed from fragments of historical writings by figures such as Leon Trotsky and Emma Goldman. These unsettling bursts of language were 'designed to be stumbled across in the course of a person's daily life', Holzer has stated. She collaborated with the graffiti artist Lady Pink on a series of paintings in the early 1980s, notably *TRUST*

VISIONS THAT DON'T FEATURE BUCKETS OF BLOOD (1983-4). David Hammons' piece of absurdist street theatre *Bliz-aard ball sale* (1983) survives only in photographs taken by Dawoud Bey, but those interested should seek out Elena Filipovic's book (MIT Press, 2017). With the support of the Public Art Fund, Pope.L recently restaged his infamous crawls across Manhattan as a group activity involving over 140 volunteers, conscientiously clad in knee and elbow protectors.

Fifth Floor

For more information on Nan Goldin's campaign against the Sackler family through the institutions it sponsors, read the mission statement of P.A.I.N. (Prescription Addiction Intervention Now) online. Other significant protest actions at institutions in recent years have been led by Decolonize this Place (specifically its Nine Weeks of Art and Action at the Whitney Museum) and the Art Not Oil coalition (which occupied the Turbine Hall of the Tate Modern in 2015). The 2014 Biennale of Sydney is remembered for protests against its sponsorship by Transfield Holdings, a private company with a minority stake in the public corporation which administers two of Australia's offshore immigrant detention centres, the same year in which activists scattered fake money across the famous atrium of the Guggenheim, New York in protest at the conditions for workers in the museum's outpost in Abu Dhabi. Culture Declares Emergency is among those groups staging actions to draw attention to the art world's implication in the climate crisis.

The man obstructing Dana Schutz's painting is the artist Parker Bright, who held a vigil in front of the work. Hannah Black's open letter to the Whitney Biennial's curators, Christopher Y. Lew and Mia Locks, published by *Artforum* on 21 March 2017 and updated with a list of co-signatories, can be read online.

Zanele Muholi's *Faces and Phases* (2006, ongoing) is an expanding archive of portraits of

South Africa's queer community. The Nam June Paik film is a recording of a 1986 variety programme *Bye Bye Kipling*, which was broadcast via a live satellite link-up of studios in Japan, Korea and the United States. It features Philip Glass, Kabuki dancers, Charlotte Moorman and Lou Reed, among others, and I wanted to squeeze it in somewhere (this jumbled gallery, which the narrator has so poorly curated, is not really the place) as a utopian example of the cross-pollination of cultures, histories and disciplines. Kerry James Marshall's *De Style* (1993) and *A Portrait of the Artist as a Shadow of His Former Self* (1980) – which in their combination of European art history and Black American experience practise a more conflicted, ambiguous exchange – were included in the American painter's acclaimed 2017 retrospective *Mastry* at the Museum of Contemporary Art, Los Angeles.

On 26 November 2019, the *New York Times* published an article titled 'Is It Time Gauguin Got Canceled?' The painter's exploitative relationships with the Polynesian teenagers that he painted as sex objects, not to mention his characterization of the local culture as savage, should make his work profoundly distasteful to contemporary audiences. That it remains popular speaks to the protections enjoyed by canonical European artists and, perhaps, the way that, in the age of film and photography, figurative paintings have lost something of their immediacy (how strange that straight men can stand in a gallery and unself-consciously gawp at Manet's *Olympia*, 1865, for example). Gauguin's excellence as a painter cannot 'redeem' his attitudes, but (good) art by its nature complicates things by resisting its own instrumentalization (which is to say, its use as propaganda, whether for good or evil). Whether or not the work of a man who was, to be blunt and to use today's terms, a racist paedophile should be shown in muse-ums, imaginary or otherwise, is for the reader to decide.

The Tunnels

Teresa Burga's *Autorretrato. Estructura. Informe, 9.6.72.* (1972) was included in *A Tale of Two Worlds. Experimental Latin American in Dialogue with the Collection* at the Museum für Moderne Kunst in Frankfurt in 2017. Created almost half a century ago, the work's presentation of state-issued and -owned medical records, ID cards and personal information reads now – as regimes across the world track citizens through their phones and the UK government trails the introduction of virus-tracing apps to break the lockdown – as startlingly prescient. The alternately beautiful, flirtatious and tortured sculptures in resin, electrical wiring, plastic foil and polyurethane foam of Alina Szapocznikow, who died in 1973 at the age of forty-seven, have recently come to greater attention outside her native Poland. The Museum of Modern Art in Warsaw has the best holdings.

A.R. Ammons' *The Snow Poems* (1977) is a good reminder to attend to what art (what the world) does to the senses before intellectualizing it: 'I do not care what anybody / thinks of anything, really: / that is to say, I have not / found the flavor of orange / juice diminished or increased / by this or that approach to / Heidegger or Harmonium: I / believe the constituency of / water has remained constant / since the Pleides: / I don't think that any / attitude I take to spider webs / will faze flies'

The Burrow

To separate out and name each of the individual works from the items of sentimental value to the narrator in this section would defeat the purpose, but mention should be made of Patrick Jolley & Reynold Reynolds' film *Burn* (2002), which was included in the group exhibition *INSIDE* at the Palais de Tokyo, Paris in 2014.

Better to finish here with a quote from Annie Ernaux's *The Years*, translated by Alison L. Strayer for Fitzcarraldo Editions: 'Like sexual desire, memory never stops. It pairs the dead with the living, real with imaginary beings, dreams with history.'

List of Illustrations

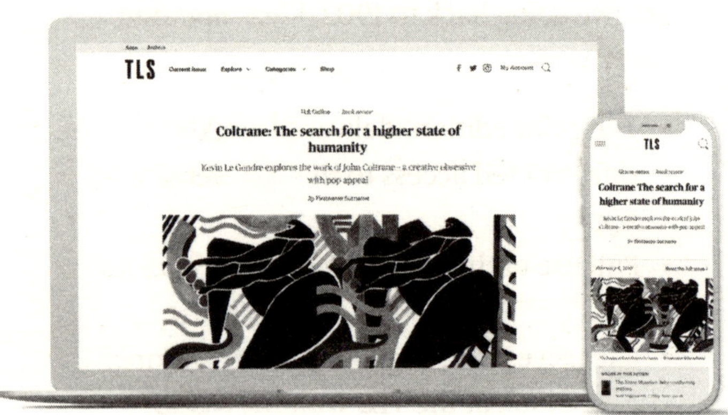

TLS

Also from TLS Books

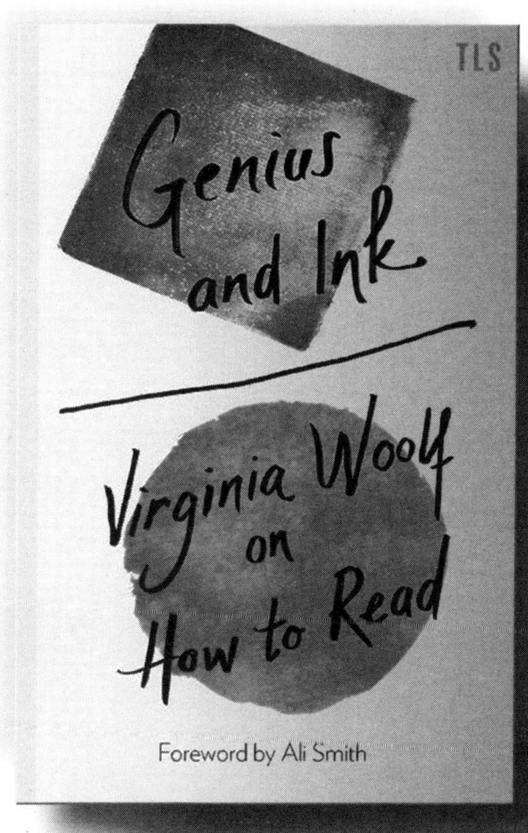

Who better to serve as a guide to great books and their authors than Virginia Woolf?

Also from TLS Books

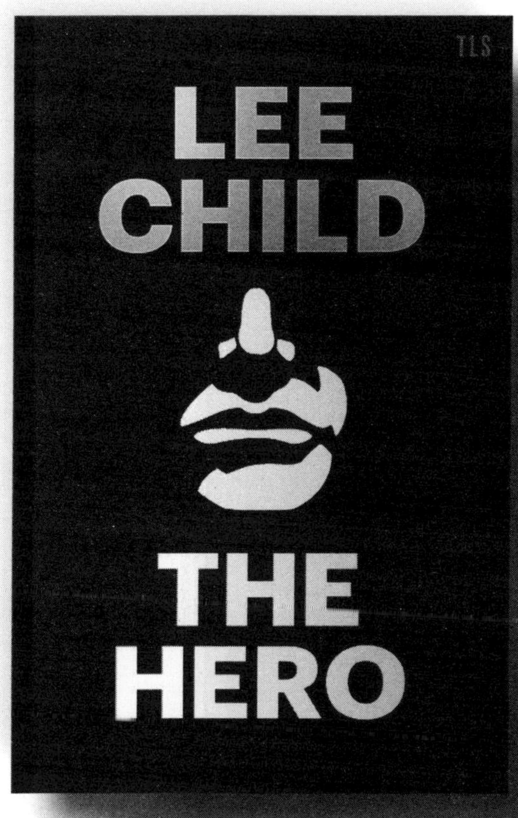

The bestselling author of the Jack Reacher
books explores what makes a hero